1,000 FACTS ABOUT THE BIBLE

BY ROBIN CURRIE AND JILL RUBALCABA FOREWORD BY JEAN-PIERRE ISBOUTS

NATIONAL GEOGRAPHIC

WASHINGTON, D.C.

TABLE OF CONTENTS

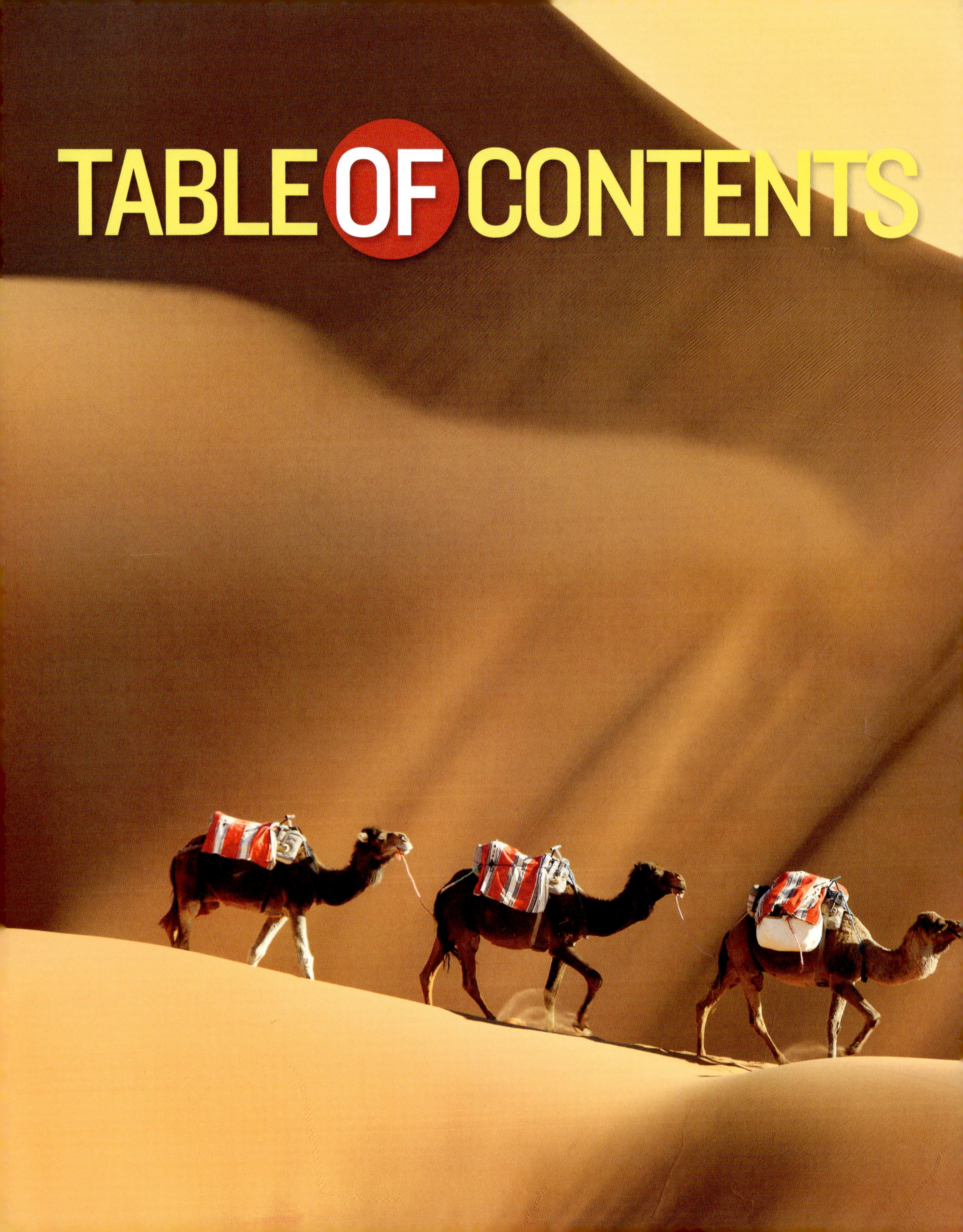

PARABOLE

Incipit prologus sancti iheronimi presbiteri in parabolas salomonis

Iungat epistola quos iungit sacerdocium: immo carta non dividat: quos xpi nectit amor. Commentarios in osee. amos. et zachariam malachiam quoque poscitis. Scripsissem: si licuisset pre valitudine. Mittitis solacia sumptuum. notarios nostros et librarios sustentans: ut vobis potissimum nostrum desudet ingenium. Et ecce ex latere frequens turba diversa poscentium: quasi aut equum sit me vobis esurientibus aliis laborare: aut in ratione dati et accepti: cuiquam preter vos obnoxius sim. Itaque longa egrotatione fractus. ne penitus hoc anno reticerem et apud vos mutus essem: tridui opus nomini vestro consecravi. interpretationem videlicet trium salomonis voluminum: masloth quod hebrei parabolas. vulgata editio proverbia vocat: coeleth. quem grece ecclesiasten. latine concionatorem possumus dicere: sirasirim. quod in linguam nostram vertitur canticum canticorum. Fertur et panaretos ihesu filii sirach liber: et alius pseudographus. qui sapientia salomonis inscribitur. Quorum priorem hebraicum reperi. non ecclesiasticum ut apud latinos: sed parabolas prenotatum. Cui iuncti erant ecclesiastes et canticum canticorum: ut similitudinem salomonis. non solum numero librorum: sed etiam materiarum genere coequaret. Secundus apud hebreos nusquam est: quia et ipse stilus grecam eloquentiam redolet: et nonnulli scriptorum veterum hunc esse iudei filonis affirmant. Sicut ergo iudith et thobie et machabeorum libros legit quidem eos ecclesia. sed inter canonicas scripturas non recipit: sic et hec duo volumina legat ad edificationem plebis: non ad auctoritatem ecclesiasticorum dogmatum confirmandam. Si cui sane septuaginta interpretum magis editio placet: habet eam a nobis olim emendatam. Neque enim nova sic cudimus: ut vetera destruamus. Et tamen cum diligentissime legerit: sciat magis nostra scripta intelligi: que non in tercium vas transfusa coacuerint: sed statim de prelo purissime commendata teste: suum saporem servaverit. Incipiunt parabole salomonis

Parabole salomonis filii david regis israel: ad sciendam sapientiam et disciplinam: ad intelligenda verba prudentie et suscipiendam eruditationem doctrine: iusticiam et iudicium et equitatem: ut detur parvulis astutia: et adolescenti scientia et intellectus. Audiens sapiens sapientior erit: et intelligens gubernacula possidebit. Animadvertet parabolam et interpretationem: verba sapientum et enigmata eorum. Timor domini principium sapientie. Sapientiam atque doctrinam stulti despiciunt. Audi fili mi disciplinam patris tui et ne dimittas legem matris tue: ut addatur gracia capiti tuo: et torques collo tuo. Fili mi si te lactaverint peccatores: ne acquiescas eis. Si dixerint veni nobiscum. insidiemur sanguini. abscondamus tediculas contra insontem frustra. deglutiamus eum sicud infernus viventem et integrum. quasi descendentem in lacum: omnem preciosam substanciam reperiemus. implebimus domus nostras spoliis. sortem mitte nobiscum. marsupium sit unum omnium nostrum: fili mi ne ambules cum eis. Prohibe pedem tuum a semitis eorum. Pedes enim illorum ad malum currunt: et festinant ut effundant sanguinem. Frustra autem iacitur rete ante oculos pennatorum. Ipsi quoque contra sanguinem suum insidiantur: et

Page from the Gutenberg Bible, ca 1454

FOREWORD

The Bible: Why is it such an important book? Why is it read by people all over the world—by one count, in more than a thousand different languages? What makes the Bible so special?

Over the centuries, a lot of writers have tried to answer these questions. Some believe that Bible stories are a guide to help us decide what is right and wrong. These authors talk about the Bible as the "ethical basis" of what it takes to be a good person. Others believe that these same stories have inspired so many beautiful works of art, music, poetry, and literature that the Bible should be considered a key source of our culture and Western civilization.

It's up to you to decide how you will use biblical stories in your life. Although the Bible was written over a period of more than 1,000 years by many different scribes, many people believe it may reveal what God has intended for people, sometimes literally and sometimes through metaphors, examples, and the lessons in the stories. For others, the stories in the Bible are messages for all time and are about how to find a path through our complicated world.

That is why an hour spent with the Bible can be such a great and uplifting experience, and why it is important to start reading the Bible at a young age. The more familiar you are with the Bible when you're young, the more informative and useful it will be when you become an adult. For thousands of years, writers, philosophers, theologians, artists, and everyday people have used lessons from the Bible in daily life—not only in a religious sense but also at work, at school, or at home, or when visiting places around the world. And that's precisely why having the facts about the Bible at your fingertips is such a wonderful idea.

Although we refer to the Bible as a single "book," the Old and New Testaments consist of around 66 individual "books." These didn't start out as bound books, of the type we use today, but as rolls of papyrus. In fact, the word "bible" is based on the Greek word *biblia,* meaning "little books." The first 39 books come from an older collection known as the Hebrew Scriptures, originally written in Hebrew and Aramaic. This is essentially the same Bible collection that is used in Jewish homes and synagogues today. Christians refer to this collection as the Old Testament.

The second part of the Bible is called the New Testament, and it contains 27 books and forms the sacred scripture of Christianity. Perhaps the most important of these are the four Gospels (from the old English phrase *good spell,* meaning "good news"), originally written in Greek. The Gospels tell us about the life and teachings of Jesus, and they were probably written in the latter part of the first century.

Whether you are Christian or Jewish, or you simply want to better understand the importance of the Bible in our modern times, *1,000 Facts About the Bible* is not only a trustworthy guide but also a very entertaining one. It will introduce you to many amazing people, countless exotic places, and scores of exciting events that will inspire you for the rest of your life.

JEAN-PIERRE ISBOUTS
Author, National Geographic's *In the Footsteps of Jesus* and *The Biblical World*

PUBLISHER'S NOTE

Inside this book, you'll find 1,000 facts about specific passages or text in the Bible as well as facts about things that happened during biblical times. At the back of *1,000 Facts About the Bible,* you'll find a section called Annotations, which identifies the Bible passages that provided the source for each of the 1,000 entries in the book. Each annotation is listed by the name of the book in the Bible from which it came, such as Exodus or Genesis; by the chapter, or section of the book; and by the verse or specific lines in the chapter. For instance, on page 23 you'll read that the first garden mentioned in the Bible is Eden. In the Annotations section, on pages 92–93, you'll see that this mention appears in Genesis 2:8—that is, the Book of Genesis, chapter 2, verse 8.

The translation of the Bible used to compile the content in this book is the New Revised Standard Version of the Bible (NRSV). We hope you'll enjoy these 1,000 facts about the Bible.

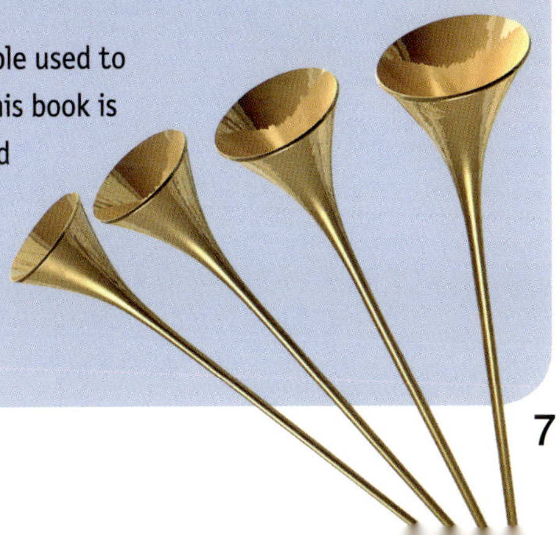

10 FAST FACTS YOU NEED TO KNOW ABOUT

1

THE BIBLE HAS MANY DIFFERENT **STORIES** ABOUT PEOPLE, SUCH AS MOSES, JESUS, AND PAUL, AND EVENTS, SUCH AS WAR, PUNISHMENT, AND MIRACLES. THE STORIES MAINLY FALL INTO **THREE CATEGORIES: HISTORY, LAW, AND LESSONS.**

2

THE BIBLE HAS **TWO MAIN PARTS** THAT COVER **THREE MAJOR ERAS: THE OLD TESTAMENT** COVERS THE AGE OF THE PATRIARCHS, OR FOREFATHERS, AND THE AGE OF ISRAEL. **THE NEW TESTAMENT** IS ABOUT THE AGE OF CHRIST.

3

Archaeologists have discovered and excavated many of the cities and towns mentioned in the Bible, and they have found **SIGNET SEALS AND INSCRIPTIONS** that directly link to people in the Bible.

4

The first Bible was a collection of writings translated into Greek starting around the third century B.C.E., and then into Latin. **TODAY THERE ARE BIBLES IN MORE THAN 1,000 LANGUAGES.**

5

The Old and New Testaments are divided into separate **books.** Each book has short **chapters** made up of **verses.** For instance, to read about the Ten Commandments, you'd look in the Old Testament Book of Exodus, chapter 20, verses 2–18, or **EXODUS 20:2–18.**

6

THE BOOKS OF THE NEW TESTAMENT WEREN'T WRITTEN TO BE PART OF THE BIBLE, BUT AS **LETTERS TO BE READ DURING CHURCH SERVICES.** IN THE FOURTH CENTURY C.E. THEY WERE OFFICIALLY ADDED TO THE CHRISTIAN BIBLE.

THE BIBLE

7

DIFFERENT RELIGIONS
ADD OR SUBTRACT
BOOKS OF THE BIBLE,
REORDER THEM, or
FOLLOW SPECIFIC TRANSLATIONS.
A religion's own Bible is called its biblical canon. "Canon" comes from the Greek word *kanon*,
MEANING "RULE" OR "MEASURING STICK."

8

The word "bible" comes from the Greek ***BIBLIA***, or
"BOOKS."
This might refer to the seaport BYBLOS, where Greek traders bought Egyptian papyrus to first make scrolls, then books.

9

In Jesus' time there were no Bibles. Instead, Jesus would have memorized the scrolls of teachers and rabbis. It is said that the
12-YEAR-OLD JESUS
COULD RECITE THE TORAH AND OTHER WRITINGS IN FORMAL HEBREW.

10

THE BIBLE WAS WRITTEN OVER A PERIOD OF ABOUT
1,000 YEARS,
ON THREE CONTINENTS,
AND
IN THREE LANGUAGES—
BY **SHEPHERDS, FISHERMEN, PHILOSOPHERS,** AND **KINGS.**
ITS UNIVERSAL MESSAGE STILL TOUCHES OUR LIVES EVERY DAY, FROM PRACTICING THE GOLDEN RULE TO DEBATING POLITICAL RIGHTS.

LANDS OF THE BIBLE

Welcome to the biblical world, spanning many centuries and three continents—Asia, Africa, and Europe. Most Bible accounts take place from Syria and Mesopotamia to Egypt and Israel, in land promised by God to Abraham in the Book of Genesis. If you study and read the Bible closely, you may find that the lands, people, and events are unforgettable.

MISSION CHURCH

The Apostle Paul took four missionary trips to preach Jesus' Gospel. On the first trip, he founded the first non-Jewish church in Antioch of Pisidia. (pages 80–81)

SPOILS OF WAR

The Arch of Titus in Rome has carved images of Jerusalem's Holy Temple being robbed by the Romans in 70 C.E. One image shows soldiers taking the lampstand and two silver trumpets. (pages 44–45)

NEW CHRISTIANS

The first person Paul converted in Macedonia was a woman. Her name was Lydia and she was a merchant who sold purple cloth. (pages 84–85)

PAUL'S JOB

The Apostle Paul was a tentmaker in Corinth. (pages 46–47)

GREAT RESCUE

To help the Israelites escape the Egyptians, God parted the Red Sea so they could cross on dry land; then he closed it, drowning the Egyptians. (pages 42–43)

DESERT WANDERING

Moses and the Israelites spent 40 years in the Sinai desert after they escaped Egypt. (pages 70–71)

MAP KEY

- From the Old Testament
- From the New Testament
- Place associated with Jesus
- Other city

PEOPLE AND PLACES 20TH CENTURY B.C.E. TO 1ST CENTURY C.E.

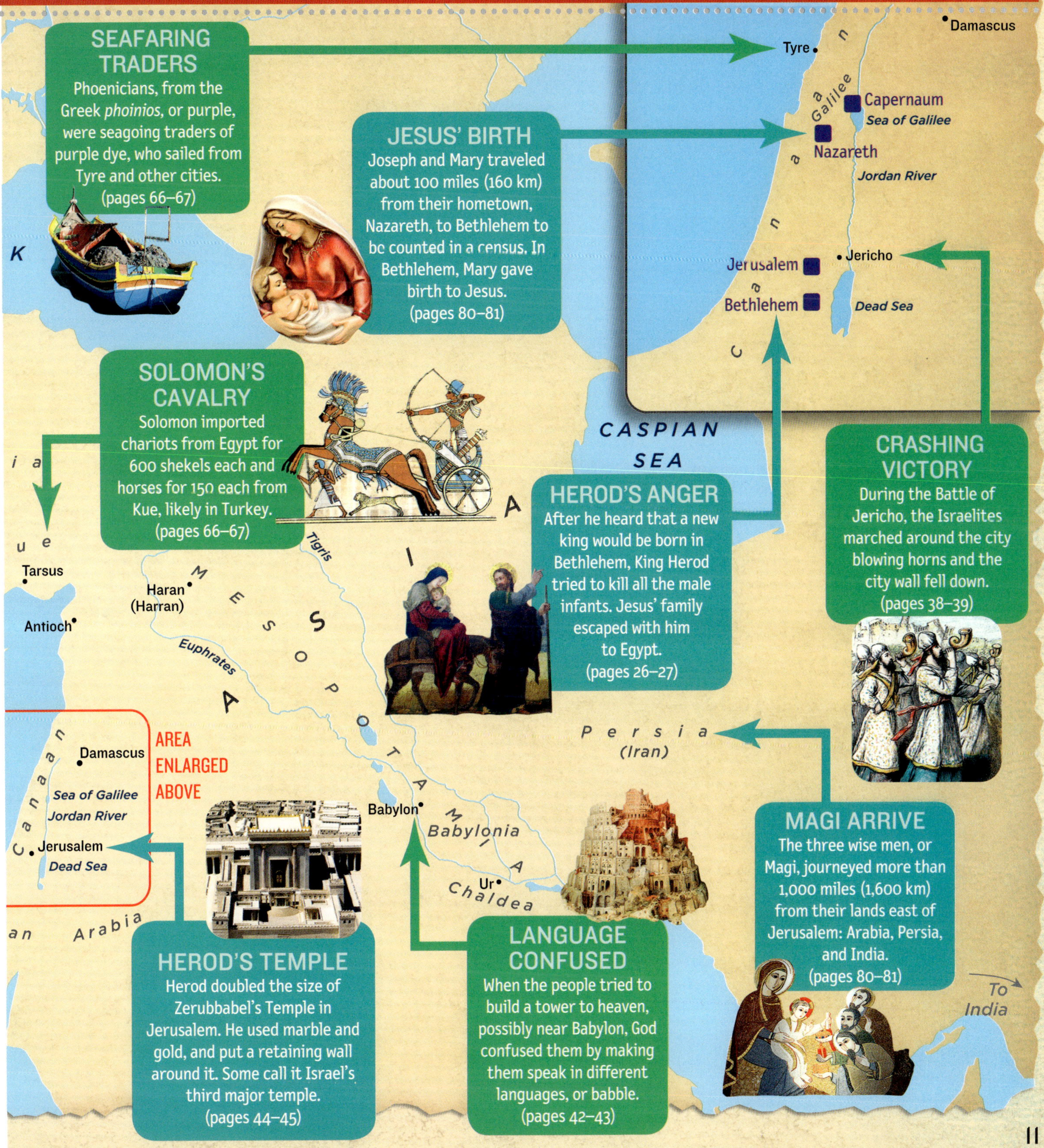

SEAFARING TRADERS

Phoenicians, from the Greek *phoinios*, or purple, were seagoing traders of purple dye, who sailed from Tyre and other cities. (pages 66–67)

JESUS' BIRTH

Joseph and Mary traveled about 100 miles (160 km) from their hometown, Nazareth, to Bethlehem to be counted in a census. In Bethlehem, Mary gave birth to Jesus. (pages 80–81)

SOLOMON'S CAVALRY

Solomon imported chariots from Egypt for 600 shekels each and horses for 150 each from Kue, likely in Turkey. (pages 66–67)

HEROD'S ANGER

After he heard that a new king would be born in Bethlehem, King Herod tried to kill all the male infants. Jesus' family escaped with him to Egypt. (pages 26–27)

CRASHING VICTORY

During the Battle of Jericho, the Israelites marched around the city blowing horns and the city wall fell down. (pages 38–39)

MAGI ARRIVE

The three wise men, or Magi, journeyed more than 1,000 miles (1,600 km) from their lands east of Jerusalem: Arabia, Persia, and India. (pages 80–81)

HEROD'S TEMPLE

Herod doubled the size of Zerubbabel's Temple in Jerusalem. He used marble and gold, and put a retaining wall around it. Some call it Israel's third major temple. (pages 44–45)

LANGUAGE CONFUSED

When the people tried to build a tower to heaven, possibly near Babylon, God confused them by making them speak in different languages, or babble. (pages 42–43)

1

CAIN AND ABEL were the first children in the Bible, sons of Adam and Eve.

2

Because they were so old, **ABRAHAM AND SARAH** laughed when God said they'd have a son. When he was born they named him Isaac, which means **"he laughs."**

3

Moses' sister, **MIRIAM,** followed her **BABY BROTHER** as he floated in a basket down the Nile, to be sure he was safe. She later became a prophet.

4

ISAAC AND REBEKAH HAD TWIN SONS, **Jacob and Esau.** ESAU AND HIS FATHER WERE CLOSE AND HUNTED TOGETHER. JACOB WAS QUIET AND CLOSE TO HIS MOTHER.

5

Sons WERE HIGHLY VALUED: "LIKE ARROWS IN THE HAND OF A WARRIOR ARE THE SONS OF ONE'S YOUTH. HAPPY IS THE MAN WHO HAS HIS QUIVER FULL OF THEM."

25 PINT-SIZE FACTS ABOUT

6

As a boy, **DAVID** cared for sheep, using his **slingshot** to kill lions and bears that came near. This skill helped him when he faced the giant Goliath.

7

WHEN HE WAS STILL A CHILD, DAVID WAS IN THE ARMY OF KING SAUL, HELPING THE ISRAELITES FIGHT AGAINST THE PHILISTINES.

8

During a battle, young David chose five stones for his slingshot, but killed the giant Goliath after smacking him in the forehead **WITH A SINGLE STONE.**

9

JEREMIAH BECAME A **PROPHET** WHEN HE WAS JUST A YOUNG BOY.

10

By eating only vegetables and drinking water, Daniel and his young friends showed King Nebuchadnezzar that this diet was healthier than meat and wine.

11

When Jesus was **12,** he was separated from his parents during a visit to Jerusalem; his parents found him in a temple, **talking to temple leaders.**

12

The proverb that begins **"The good leave an inheritance for their children's children"** shows the importance of providing for your family.

13

David was a **SKILLED MUSICIAN** when he was young. He lifted King Saul from bad moods with beautiful melodies from his **harp.**

14
The Book of Matthew says that **JESUS HAD FOUR BROTHERS:** James, Joseph, Judas, and Simon. **He also had sisters,** but they are neither named nor numbered.

15
JACOB HAD A FAVORITE SON, **Joseph.** WHEN JACOB GAVE JOSEPH A BEAUTIFUL COAT, IT MADE THE OTHER 11 BOYS JEALOUS, AND SO THEY PLOTTED TO GET RID OF HIM.

16
IT WAS THE ADVICE OF A YOUNG GIRL THAT LED NAAMAN, COMMANDER OF THE SYRIAN ARMY, TO SEEK A CURE FOR HIS LEPROSY THROUGH THE PROPHET ELISHA.

17

Abraham prepared to offer his son, Isaac, on the altar as a sacrifice to God. **God spared the boy at the last second; a ram was sacrificed instead.**

CHILDREN

18
Some books of the New Testament are **LETTERS** from the Apostle Paul to Timothy. Paul was Timothy's mentor, or adviser, starting when Timothy was a boy.

19

God made Josiah king **WHEN HE WAS EIGHT YEARS OLD,** replacing Josiah's father and grandfather, who had made God angry with their evil ways.

20
WHEN SAMUEL WAS A LITTLE BOY, HE LIVED AND WORKED IN THE TEMPLE. Every year his mother, Hannah, would bring him a **NEW COAT** that she'd made for him.

21
The Bible stated that **children must love, respect, and obey their parents**—or the children would die.

25
The expression **"Spare the rod and spoil the child"** comes from the Bible. People then believed harsh discipline was required to raise good children.

22
Instead of going to school, **CHILDREN BECAME APPRENTICES** to learn a job. Paul praised Timothy for being a good apprentice, as he spread God's word.

23
The disciples thought children wasted Jesus' precious time and sent them away. **JESUS DISAGREED AND TOLD THE DISCIPLES TO LET THE CHILDREN COME.**

24
THE DISCIPLE PAUL'S LIFE WAS SAVED BY HIS YOUNG NEPHEW, WHO UNCOVERED A ROMAN PLOT TO ARREST AND KILL PAUL.

1
The first family in the Bible was Eve and Adam's family. Their sons were Cain and Abel; they also had a son named Seth and other children.

2
Though Adam had one wife, some of his descendants had **more than one**—a practice known as polygamy.

3
If his brother died without a son, a man was required to **marry the brother's widow.**

4
If a family had many wives and children, **the firstborn son** inherited the father's wealth, even if his mother wasn't the father's favorite wife.

5
Deuteronomy warned against a king having **too many wives** "or else his heart will turn away."

6
Did Solomon listen to God's warning against too many wives? **He had 700!**

7
In Psalms, God promises to **bless** not just individuals but **generations.**

8
Abraham is known as the father of many nations—his descendants would be as **numerous as the stars in the sky** and the sand on the seashore.

9
Abraham and Sarah were very old and wanted **a child.** So Sarah offered her servant Hagar to have a baby with Abraham, named Ishmael.

10
Later, Sarah and Abraham did have a son, Isaac. **Abraham was 100!**

11
To prove his obedience to God, Abraham was prepared to do anything—even **sacrifice his beloved son** Isaac. An angel stopped him.

12
A hungry Esau begged his younger brother Jacob for a **bowl of stew.** Jacob gave it to him in exchange for Esau's inheritance as the oldest son.

13
To prevent Esau from murdering Jacob for taking his inheritance, their mother, Rebekah, **sent Jacob to work for her brother,** Laban.

14
Jacob **worked for seven years** to win the hand of his uncle Laban's daughter Rachel—but was given her sister, Leah, instead.

15
Jacob worked **seven more years** to have Rachel as his second wife.

16
According to the New Testament, taking care of people outside your own family is important, especially **orphans and widows** without families.

17
Jacob had a big family—four wives, one daughter, and twelve sons. His sons' descendants became the **12 tribes of Israel.**

18
Jacob showed that Joseph was his favorite son by giving him **a coat.** His other sons were jealous and sold Joseph into slavery.

19
One commandment is about family: **"Honor your father and mother."**

20
When God called Abraham to the **Promised Land,** he also called his descendants to become a great nation.

21
According to the New Testament, a person who does not take care of his or her family is worse than someone who **does not believe in God.**

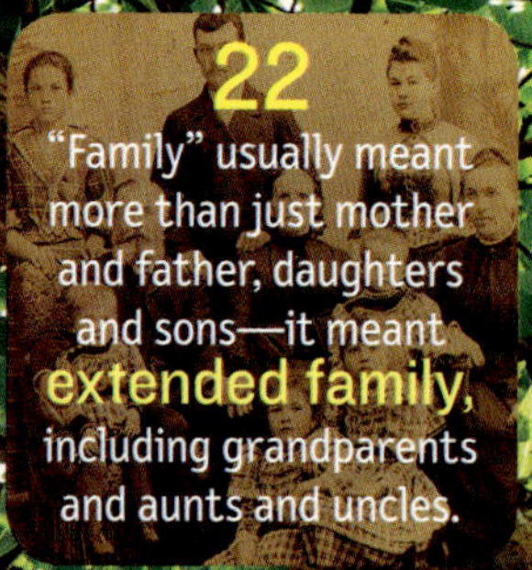

22
"Family" usually meant more than just mother and father, daughters and sons—it meant **extended family,** including grandparents and aunts and uncles.

23
In the Bible, **children are special!** "Like arrows in the hand of a warrior are the children . . . Blessed is the man who fills his quiver with them!"

24
God saved **Noah and his whole family,** saying "you shall come into the ark, you, your sons, your wife, and your sons' wives with you."

25
Noah's grandfather, Methuselah, lived for **969 years.**

26
Noah had three sons: Ham, Shem, and Japheth. According to Genesis, the **whole human family** is descended from them.

27
Moses, his brother, Aaron, and his sister, Miriam, were all **prophets.**

28
The father of Moses and Aaron was Amram, who **lived to be 137.**

29
Amram married his father's sister, Jochebed. That means **the mother of Moses and Aaron was also their great-aunt.**

30
Aaron was the first high priest of the Israelites, and **his sons and their sons** also became priests.

31
Joshua spoke for his entire family when he said to the Israelites: "[A]s for me and my household, **we will serve the Lord."**

50 Facts About FAMILY Matters

32
Lydia was the first convert to Christianity in what is modern Greece. When she was baptized, her **whole household** was baptized, too.

33
David was a great king but had a hard time with his family. One of his sons, Absalom, **killed his stepbrother** and rebelled against David.

34
When a man married, he had to **"leave and cleave,"** as the King James Bible puts it—leave his father and mother, and cleave, or bond, to his **wife.**

35
A passage in Proverbs says "a true friend sticks closer than one's nearest kin," possibly meaning that **a good friend can be like a family member.**

36
To find Isaac a wife, the servant Eliezer traveled to the family homeland. Rebekah offered **water** to both him and his ten camels; he knew he had found her.

37
Even though Isaac and Rebekah were **first cousins,** they were married.

38
Esau married two Canaanite women, then married someone **his parents approved of—** his cousin Mahalath.

39
Tamar married one of Judah's sons, who died, and then another son, who also died. Later, she had a child with Judah. That child's descendants included **King David.**

40
Abraham was a **patriarch,** a man who ruled a family or tribe.

41
A patriarch's wife was a **matriarch,** such as Abraham's wife Sarah.

42
Esther, Queen of Persia with King Ahasuerus, was **both cousin and adopted daughter** of Mordecai, a trusted confidant to the king.

43
David's first wife was Michal, daughter of King Saul. The Bible says Michal loved David, **but it doesn't say if he loved her.**

44
Michal never had children and was referred to as the **"daughter of Saul"** rather than the "wife of David."

45
The New Testament says: "Honor your father and your mother, **so that your days may be long** in the land that the Lord . . . is giving you."

46
The New Testament warns parents: **"[D]o not provoke your children to anger,** but bring them up in the discipline . . . of the Lord."

47
Jesus had four brothers—James, Joseph, Judas, and (for a break from all those J names) Simon. He also had sisters, but the Bible doesn't give their names.

48
The Bible says that **Jesus' father was God—**not Mary's husband, Joseph.

49
John the Baptist was Jesus' second cousin. Their mothers were **cousins.**

50
Matthew and Luke said Jesus was in the royal line of King David. Matthew counted **28 generations** from David to Jesus.

15 UPLIFTING FACTS

❶ The word for "angel" in Hebrew is *malak;* the English word has roots in the Greek word *angelos.* Both mean "messenger."

❷ In most pictures of angels, they have wings. In the Bible, angels are not described with wings.

❸ Two angels visited Lot to warn him to leave the city of Sodom, which God was about to destroy because the people had been wicked.

❹ Angels often took human form. Abraham had lunch with three travelers, some of whom turned out to be angels.

❺ After the slave Hagar conceived a child with Abraham, an angel told her the baby would be a boy and that she should name him Ishmael.

❻ Angels live forever. They generally don't marry and don't have children, although Genesis names one kind of heavenly being that did: the nephilim.

❼ Archangels are angels of high rank, like Michael, called "a great prince," who protected the people. Most angels are not given names in the Scriptures.

"Annunciatory Angel," by Fra Angelico, 1450–1455

ABOUT ANGELS

8 Before **Samson** was born, an angel told his mother that she would bear a son and that **he must promise never to cut his hair.** His vow would make him stronger than any other man.

9 **Gideon doubted his ability to lead the Israelites** in battle against the Midianites, but an angel encouraged him by calling him **a mighty man of valor.**

10 In the Bible, Jesus said that **children have angels who "always see the face of my Father in heaven,"** but the idea of "guardian angels" didn't develop until the fourth or fifth century C.E.

11 **The archangel Gabriel** appeared to Mary to tell her she would be the **mother of Jesus.**

12 An angel appeared to Mary's husband, Joseph, **in a dream.** "Get up," he said, "take the child and his mother and flee to Egypt . . . **for Herod is going to search for the child to kill him."**

13 **"Do not forget to show hospitality to strangers,"** the Book of Hebrews advised, "for by doing that **some have entertained angels without knowing it."**

14 After Jesus was born, **angels visited shepherds in the fields** to tell them the news. Their opening words were what angels often said when they appeared to humans: **"Do not be afraid."**

15 **The Book of Revelation did not call them angels** but described heavenly beings with **six wings, covered with eyes,** and proclaiming, "Holy, holy, holy is the Lord God Almighty . . ."

25 ROYAL AND REGAL FACTS ABOUT

1 **Queen Esther's** life is recorded in the Book of Esther, **the only book that does not mention God or prayer.**

2 **Josiah** might have been the youngest king of Israel. **He was just eight years old when he came to the throne.**

3 IN THE BIBLE, THE HEBREW WORD *MELEK* AND THE GREEK *BASILEUS* ARE USED FOR **KING**—SOMEONE WHO HOLDS **SUPREME POWER** IN A NATION OR CITY.

4 **WICKED KING AHAB,** THE SON OF OMRI, KILLED, STOLE, WORSHIPPED IDOLS, AND **"DID EVIL IN THE SIGHT OF THE LORD, MORE THAN ALL WHO WERE BEFORE HIM."**

5 Babylon's **King Nebuchadnezzar** was a great builder—and destroyer. He likely captured Jerusalem in 597 B.C.E. and destroyed Solomon's Temple in 586 B.C.E.

6 Instead of being ruled by judges, the Israelites wanted a king, like other nations. **Their first king was the handsome SAUL.**

7 

SAUL regularly disobeyed God, so God replaced him with **DAVID.**

8 WHEN WISE MEN TOLD **HEROD** THEY HAD COME TO VISIT JESUS, THE NEWBORN "KING OF THE JEWS," HE ORDERED **ALL YOUNG BOYS EXECUTED,** TO KILL HIS COMPETITION.

9 When she visited King Solomon, the **Queen of Sheba** brought gifts of camels ladened with **spices, precious stones, and 120 talents, or units, of gold.**

10 **David** is often called Israel's greatest king. **HIS DESCENDANTS RULED FOR 400 YEARS.** As a boy in Saul's army he had killed the enemy giant **Goliath.**

11 **Jezebel** was Ahab's queen and was a good match for him. The Bible says when she died, **she was eaten by dogs.**

12 **Pontius Pilate** ORDERED A SIGN PLACED ON JESUS' CROSS WITH THESE WORDS IN HEBREW, LATIN, AND GREEK: **"JESUS OF NAZARETH, THE KING OF THE JEWS."**

13

Impressed by his miracles, some of the early followers of Jesus wanted to make him their **king.**

14

To capture Canaan, JOSHUA had to defeat 31 kings, INCLUDING KINGS OF THE HITTITES, AMORITES, CANAANITES, PERIZZITES, HIVITES, AND JEBUSITES.

15

I Kings and 2 Kings were originally one single book of the Bible. THEY RECORD WHAT HAPPENED TO THE MONARCHY IN ISRAEL AFTER THE REIGN OF DAVID.

16

KING JABIN OF HAZOR was an important ruler **defeated by Joshua**, Moses' successor, as he led the Israelites to conquer Canaan, their Promised Land.

17

JUST BEFORE HIS DEATH, JESUS' CAPTORS MOCKED HIS CLAMS TO KINGSHIP BY PLACING A CROWN OF THORNS ON HIS HEAD.

KINGS AND QUEENS

18

Just before he was slain and his kingdom overthrown, Babylon's **KING BELSHAZZAR** saw a disembodied hand writing a message saying HIS TIME WAS UP.

19

MERNEPTAH was the first pharaoh of Egypt to mention Israel in a written historical document created on a stone slab.

20

Commissioned by James I of England, the **KING JAMES BIBLE** was the first official translation of the Bible into English.

21

IN THE BOOK OF REVELATION, JOHN HAD A VISION OF A RIDER ON A WHITE HORSE WITH WRITING ON HIS ROBE AND THIGH: "KING OF KINGS AND LORD OF LORDS."

22

After Solomon died, Israel split into two: One group of tribes refused David's grandson **REHOBOAM** as the new king; the other group agreed to follow him.

23

THE BIBLE OFTEN DOESN'T TELL US THE NAMES OF THE WIVES OF KINGS.

24

AFTER ISRAEL SPLIT, **JERUSALEM** STAYED THE CAPITAL OF THE NEW SOUTHERN KINGDOM OF JUDAH. **SAMARIA** LATER BECAME THE CAPITAL OF THE NEW NORTHERN KINGDOM.

25

"For God is the King of all the earth," it reads in Psalms. "God reigns over the nations; God is seated on his holy THRONE."

15 LUXURIOUS FACTS

1 **Palaces** in biblical times were more than a home for the king. They were **storage areas for the grain collected as taxes, and military and government headquarters.**

2 **King Solomon's Temple** had floors, walls, doors, and statues inlaid with gold, and his palace was filled with **beautiful stonework.**

3 **King Nebuchadnezzar** liked to do his heavy thinking while **pacing the roof of his royal palace.** From this vantage point, he overlooked the city of Babylon.

4 Solomon built **both a palace and a temple.**

5 King Hiram of Tyre **sent building materials, carpenters, and stonemasons** to David and Solomon to help them build palaces for themselves and a temple for God.

6 The center of many palaces was the **throne room,** where the king received guests or judged disputes. In Solomon's palace, **giant columns stood on each side of its entrance.**

7 **Herod the Great,** one of the Bible's most celebrated builders, constructed **his palace, Herodium,** around 24 B.C.E. on a hilltop with beautiful views of the desert and mountains beyond.

Detail from "Queen of Sheba Before Solomon," by Nikolaus Knüpfer, 1640s

ABOUT PALACES

8 Some palaces boasted **pools and fountains.** Because palaces were in the desert, such lavish use of precious water was a **display of extreme wealth and power.**

9 Palace walls were sometimes painted with **fake windows** to give the illusion of looking out at gorgeous landscapes. **Archaeologists found a "window" in Herod's palace, Herodium,** in 2008.

10 Herod even had **saunas** built in the bathhouses at his palaces at Jericho and Masada.

11 When Solomon gave audience in his throne room, **he rested his feet on a footstool made of solid gold.**

12 **King Solomon** had foreign wives—700 princesses and 300 concubines—who worshipped foreign gods. To try to avoid God's wrath for marrying outside the faith, **Solomon built them palaces far from God's Temple.**

13 Herod the Great's palace-fortress **Machaerus** was fortified with thick walls and **three watchtowers.**

14 **Omri,** the sixth king of Israel, built a palace in Samaria nicknamed the **"Ivory House."** He used ivory for the furniture, the walls, and even the beds.

15 The palace-fortress **Masada,** also fortified by Herod the Great, was built on a waterless plateau. Workers created **cisterns to capture rainwater** for drinking and to fill pools and baths.

15 FLOWERING FACTS

1 Gardens of vegetables, flowers, and fruit trees were often **surrounded by stone walls.** Proverbs told of a lazy man whose wall broke down; thorns overgrew his vineyard.

2 Before the **destruction of Sodom and Gomorrah,** Lot found refuge in **the plain east of the Jordan River,** which "was well watered, like the garden of the Lord."

3 Located at the foot of the Mount of Olives, **Gethsemane means "oil press" in Aramaic,** the language Jesus spoke.

4 **God had rules** for how gardens could be used. In the Book of Isaiah, God warned the people that "I will repay" acts such as **"sacrificing in gardens and offering incense on bricks."**

5 Jesus would visit the **Garden of Gethsemane** in Jerusalem to talk to God. **Judas betrayed Jesus by leading guards to find him there** as he prayed.

6 **Watchmen might stand guard** over a garden or field. The Book of Isaiah mentions a watchman's hut in a field of **cucumbers.**

7 **Noah was the first human in the Bible to plant a vineyard.** Throughout the Bible are rules for tending a vineyard and **sharing its harvest with others,** especially the poor.

ABOUT GARDENS

Detail from "The Temptation in the Garden of Eden," by Jan Brueghel the Elder, ca 1600

8 The first garden mentioned in the Bible is Eden. Many believed it was located in the area of the Tigris and Euphrates Rivers.

9 When Naboth refused to sell his vineyard to Ahab, the king's wife, Jezebel, had Naboth stoned to death so that the king could have it.

10 Gardens were sometimes near burial places. After the Crucifixion, Jesus' body was buried in a new tomb in Golgotha.

11 When Manasseh, King of Judah, died, he was buried with his ancestors in his palace garden, in or near Jerusalem.

12 In the Book of Amos, God promised to bring his people back from exile to a time of plenty. "They shall plant vineyards and drink their wine; they shall make gardens and eat their fruit."

13 At the beginning of the Book of Esther, King Ahasuerus threw a party in his palace garden that went on for seven days. "The garden had hangings of white and blue linen, fastened . . . to silver rings on marble pillars."

14 After God sent Adam and Eve out from the Garden of Eden, he placed armed cherubim at the garden's entrance.

15 In Jerusalem, the "King's Garden" was near the Pool of Siloam. When Nebuchadnezzar conquered the city, its defenders fled past the garden as they tried to escape.

25 BEASTLY FACTS

1 God challenged Job's faith with a FIRE-BREATHING DRAGON.

2 THE WICKED AND RUTHLESS KING HEROD AGRIPPA failed to praise God. For that fatal mistake he was eaten alive by worms.

3 Jesus once spoke about how wealth makes people corrupt: "IT IS EASIER FOR A CAMEL TO GO THROUGH THE EYE OF A needle than for SOMEONE WHO IS RICH TO ENTER THE KINGDOM OF GOD."

4 Today unicorns are imagined as peaceful creatures, but in biblical times they were considered the fiercest, fastest creatures on Earth.

5 DAVID, SOLOMON, AND JESUS all humbly rode into Jerusalem ON ANIMALS—either a mule, donkey, or "a colt, the foal of a donkey."

6 TO REPAY JOB for the series of trials God put him through, God gave him 14,000 SHEEP, 6,000 CAMELS, 1,000 OXEN, and 1,000 DONKEYS.

7 In the BOOK OF REVELATION, Death rode a pale green horse and was given authority to kill— BY SWORD, OR FAMINE, OR PLAGUE, OR WILD BEAST.

8 To please God, priests slaughtered animals, splashing blood on the sides of the altar. THEN THEY BURNED THE CARCASSES AS AN OFFERING.

9 According to the Bible, Jesus cured a man POSSESSED BY DEMONS by CASTING THE DEMONS INTO A HERD OF pigs.

10 Camels, called "SHIPS OF THE DESERT," carried people and goods long distances.

11 Blown like a trumpet, the ram's horn, or shofar, called people to WAR OR WORSHIP.

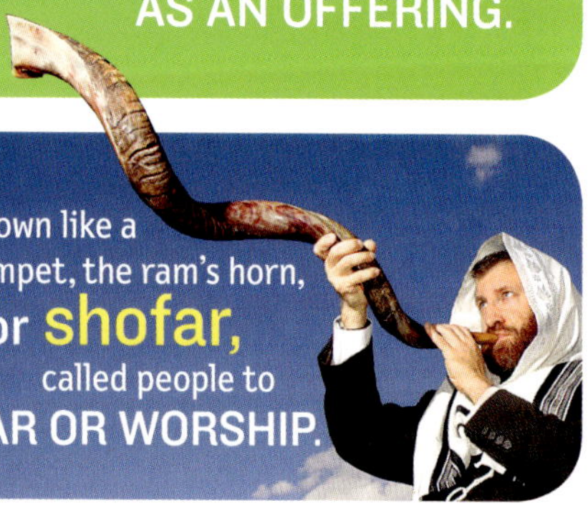

12 IN THE BOOK OF JOB, A MYSTERIOUS BEAST CALLED the behemoth MADE AN APPEARANCE. WAS IT A HIPPOPOTAMUS? AN ELEPHANT? OR A MYTHICAL MONSTER? No one knows for sure.

13 Balaam whipped his donkey for veering off the road, lying down, and trying to brush Balaam off his back. GOD GAVE THE DONKEY SPEECH SO IT COULD COMPLAIN.

ABOUT ANIMALS

14

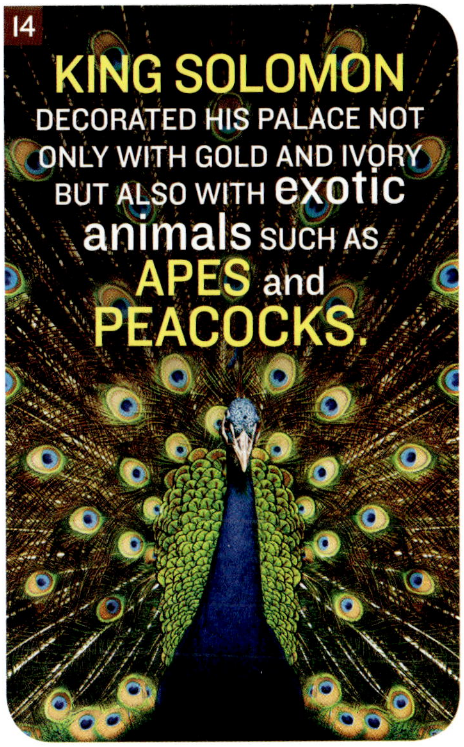

KING SOLOMON DECORATED HIS PALACE NOT ONLY WITH GOLD AND IVORY BUT ALSO WITH **exotic animals** SUCH AS **APES and PEACOCKS.**

15

Jackals—wild doglike animals—were feared in the ancient world because they ATE THE DEAD AND DYING ON THE BATTLEFIELD.

16

KING SOLOMON OWNED **12,000** HORSES. PERHAPS THEY WERE HOUSED IN STABLES LIKE THE ONES ARCHAEOLOGISTS FOUND AT THE SITE CALLED MEGIDDO.

17

When the **KING** tossed the ever faithful Daniel INTO A DEN OF **LIONS,** God sealed the lions' mouths shut. **DANIEL SURVIVED UNHARMED.**

18

An omen appeared in the **Book of Revelation.** It was a **red dragon** with seven heads, ten horns, and a crown on each head. IT SWEPT THE STARS OUT OF THE SKY WITH ITS TAIL.

19

TWO BEARS MAULED **42** BOYS WHO WERE TAUNTING ELISHA, CALLING HIM **"baldy."**

20

IN THE CASE OF AN **UNSOLVED MURDER,** ELDERS OF A TOWN WERE TOLD TO BREAK A COW'S NECK, THEN TO WASH THEIR HANDS OVER IT, DECLARING THEIR **innocence.**

21

When the Israelites complained that there was no meat, God surrounded them in **quail**—THREE FEET (90 CM) DEEP AND AS FAR AS THE EYE COULD SEE.

22

The **sneaky snake** in the Garden of Eden tricked Eve into eating the forbidden fruit. THAT ONE BITE MEANT SHE AND ADAM HAD TO LEAVE THE GARDEN.

23

IN BIBLICAL TIMES, THE TENTS OF COMMON PEOPLE WERE OFTEN SEPARATED INTO ROOMS BY CURTAINS MADE OF GOAT HAIR.

24

One PROVERB suggests that you **"GO TO THE ANT, YOU LAZYBONES,"** to see what **REAL WORKERS** look like.

25

EAGLES symbolized leadership and strength. Isaiah says that "those who hope in the Lord . . . they shall mount up with wings of eagles."

15 BOUNCING BIBLICAL

❶ Two women told Solomon they were mother to the same baby, so he suggested **splitting the child in half.** One of them gave up her claim to save the baby's life. Solomon knew she was **the real mother.**

❷ Isaac's wife, **Rebekah,** gave birth to twins who would fight for much of their lives. Even when they were born, **Jacob was gripping Esau's foot.**

❸ After he heard that **a new king would be born** in Bethlehem, **King Herod** tried to kill all the male infants. Jesus' family escaped with him to **Egypt.**

❹ In biblical times, newborn babies were immediately **bathed and rubbed with salt,** probably to toughen their skin.

❺ When Jesus was born, Mary wrapped him snugly in strips of cloth called **swaddling clothes** and laid him in a manger—a container for feeding farm animals.

❻ Christmas nativity scenes often show **the wise men** visiting the newborn Jesus. But by the time they got there, he might have been **as old as two.**

❼ Everybody knows Jesus was born on Christmas Day, **December 25,** right? **That date didn't come from the Bible;** it was chosen later by the Christian church.

"Madonna and Child," by Sassoferrato, 17th century

BABY FACTS

❽ **When a boy was 40 days old and a girl 80 days old,** Jewish mothers offered a temple sacrifice of two turtledoves or two pigeons. Jesus' mother did the same.

❾ Because his mother had promised him to God, **Samuel** was brought to live with the high priest Eli **as soon as his mother stopped nursing him.**

❿ Just like many grandmothers today, **Ruth helped raise her grandson Obed.**

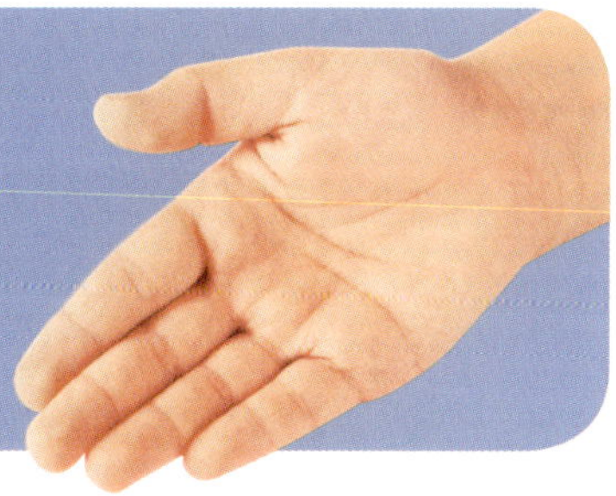

⓫ As **Rachel** was dying during childbirth, she named her son Ben-oni, **"son of my sorrow."** Her husband, Jacob, changed the name to Benjamin, **"son of my right hand."**

⓬ On the day Isaac's mother, Sarah, stopped nursing him, Abraham held a **great feast** for the child. **Sarah banished Isaac's half brother, Ishmael, from attending.**

⓭ In the Book of Psalms, **children are honored as a gift from the Lord.**

⓮ Hannah promised God that if he gave her a son, the boy would **never drink wine or cut his hair.** She bore the future prophet Samuel, meaning **"I have asked him of the Lord."**

⓯ Jesus approved of **crying babies** in the temple, saying: "From the mouths of little children and infants, you have created **praise."**

1 Before the Bible, King Hammurabi drew up the Code of Hammurabi in the 18th century B.C.E. Some of its 272 laws are like those in the Bible. It was inscribed on a tall stone slab.

2 Prebiblical laws in ancient Mesopotamia indicate that a punishment should be equal to the crime; this is similar to "an eye for an eye" in the Bible.

3 "TESTAMENT" MEANS "COVENANT" OR "CONTRACT."

4 The Old Testament tells about God's early Law, centuries before Jesus' birth. The New Testament is about Jesus' and the Apostles' teachings.

5 The first five books in the Old Testament contain many laws, commandments, and rules God gave the Israelites.

6 The first five books are called the Pentateuch, or "five books." Jews also call them the Torah, or "instruction."

7 Among God's earliest rules were the Ten Commandments, which he gave to Moses on stone tablets. They are also called Ten Words, or Ten Sayings.

8 One interpretation of the Ten Commandments: Honor God; Don't worship idols; Don't take God's name in vain; Honor the Sabbath; Honor your parents; Don't kill; Don't commit adultery; Don't steal; Don't lie; and Don't want someone else's things.

9 GOD INSTRUCTED MOSES TO BUILD A SPECIAL BOX TO HOLD THE TEN COMMANDMENTS. CALLED THE ARK OF THE COVENANT, IT WAS COVERED IN GOLD AND HAD ANGELS ON THE LID.

10 At first, the Ark of the Covenant was sheltered in a sacred tent called the Tabernacle.

11 The Law of Moses combines the Ten Commandments and the other rules God gave Moses on Mount Sinai, including how to treat your neighbor.

12 After Moses died, the Jews put all the laws of the Old Testament into one document, called the Mishnah, one of the first written records of the oral traditions.

13 There are 365 Old Testament laws about what not to do—the same as the number of days in a year.

14 There are 248 Old Testament laws about what to do—the total number of bones and organs people thought the human body contained.

15 Before the Ten Commandments, God gave six similar laws to Adam in the Garden of Eden. A seventh, calling for a court system, was added after Noah's Flood.

16 Moses had so much work judging the people's legal disputes that he had to get assistants to help.

17 For those who strictly followed the Ten Commandments, there was no work at all on the Sabbath.

18 Cloaks were precious. If a man gave his cloak to another man to cover a debt, the new owner had to return it before sundown.

19 Some laws protected natural resources. To help the soil, you could plant a field for six years, then you had to let it rest for a year.

20 God commanded people to celebrate the Festival of Unleavened Bread, called Passover today, to honor the Israelites' escape from Egypt.

21 Moses got so angry when people worshipped a golden calf instead of God that he smashed the first set of the Ten Commandments. God replaced it.

22 People were allowed to eat only "clean" animals. "Unclean" animals were carnivores or scavengers that might pass on diseases.

23 IT WAS FORBIDDEN TO EAT BEES.

24 Healthy homes were required by law. Walls had to be scraped clean—no mold or mildew allowed!

25 Health laws required cleaning clothes and bedding that had touched a sick person.

26 Only on the Day of Atonement could the high priest enter the innermost room of the Tabernacle to make up for the people's sins.

27 Farmers had to leave some crops on the edges of their fields for the poor.

28 No bearing a grudge or taking revenge was allowed. Even Jesus said in his last words: "Father forgive them, for they know not what they do."

29 Sorcery, fortune-telling, tarot cards, horoscopes, and channeling spirits were all forbidden.

30 GROOMING LAWS SAID THAT MEN WEREN'T ALLOWED TO SHAVE, AND WOMEN WEREN'T ALLOWED TO CUT THEIR HAIR.

31 The Book of Leviticus forbid changing God's creations, such as tattooing your skin or crossbreeding animals.

32 When mourning a loved one's death, you weren't allowed to hurt yourself by tearing your skin or making a bald spot on your head.

33 There were laws for practically everything and everyone, including "don't engage a dead person in a conversation."

34 Priests could not mess up their hair or tear their clothes.

35 Laws were different for buying or selling property inside a walled city and in a village without walls.

75 FACTS ABOUT

LAWS AND COMMANDMENTS

36 DRINKING BLOOD WAS AGAINST THE LAW.

37 Deuteronomy includes some changes to the laws God gave Moses on Mount Sinai. New kings were given the laws so they'd know their limits.

38 The word of at least two witnesses was required to convict someone accused of a crime.

39 Some laws must have been hard to obey, such as: Do not panic when retreating from a battle.

40 If an army lay siege to a city, the Bible allowed chopping down trees to build blockades. But not fruit trees: Those were saved for their fruit.

41 An ox and a donkey couldn't be yoked together to plow a field. Because of their different sizes and strengths, they'd both be injured.

42 If a person found a bird's nest in the road, it was legal to take the eggs, but not the mother bird.

43 Deuteronomy had safety rules. You had to build a wall, like a railing, around your roof so people wouldn't fall off.

44 The law required you to dig toilets outside the army camp. (Probably a good law!)

45 One law to help the hungry said that you could go into your neighbor's fields and eat your fill but not carry any out.

46 THE OLD TESTAMENT HAS LAWS THAT PROTECT ANIMALS.

47 The Book of Judges told stories of biblical judges. These were often military leaders God sent to help the Israelites fight foreign rulers.

48 Samson, a judge, had supernatural strength because of a vow to God that he would never cut his hair. He tore apart a lion with his bare hands.

49 To make a contract in biblical times, you just took off your sandal and handed it to the other person.

50 Hospitality was not just nice, it was the law. You had to offer water, food, and shelter to friends, strangers, and even enemies and their animals.

51 Kings did not have the authority to make new religious laws—only God did.

52 Kings were not above God's law. King Ahab died a violent death for killing his neighbor, stealing his land, and worshipping idols.

53 PSALM 19 SAID THE LAW IS SWEETER THAN HONEY, MORE DESIRABLE THAN GOLD.

54 Rules for eating sweets were easy to follow: You should eat only enough so that you wouldn't vomit.

55 The Bible commanded justice for the poor, and even suggested that those who didn't stand up for the poor were wicked.

56 The law of the Medes and the Persians in the Old Testament stated if the king signed a law, it couldn't be changed.

57 It was Old Testament law to use salt when performing sacrifices on animals.

58 Old Testament law forbade creating idols, so pictures of living people or animals weren't drawn. Even Herod did not put his face on coins.

59 NEW TESTAMENT LAW SAID NOT TO MAKE A BIG DEAL ABOUT THE GOOD DEEDS YOU PERFORM.

60 The Apostles Matthew and Luke said, "Do to others as you would have them do to you." Every major religion has this law, often called the Golden Rule.

61 The Gospel of Matthew warned: Beware of wolves in sheep's clothing—that means watch out for someone who pretends to be nice, but who is up to no good.

62 The Gospel of Matthew said that if you ask you shall receive. In turn, the Gospel of Luke commanded a person to give to every man what he asks.

63 Even Jesus had to pay taxes. It was the law.

64 Jesus said that the two most important laws in the Bible were love God with all your heart and soul and mind, and love your neighbor as you would yourself.

65 In biblical times, people presented their own cases to the judge, without lawyers. When Jesus went on trial, he stayed silent until a judge told him to speak.

66 The Gospel of Matthew said that if someone hit you on the cheek, you should offer him the other cheek instead of taking revenge.

67 The Book of Romans advised: Love your enemies.

68 The New Testament said to "be" many things: wise as a serpent, harmless as a dove, thankful, patient, sober, cheerful, steadfast, understanding, unmovable, obedient, and courteous.

69 Some commands explained how to give, who to give to, who not to give to, what to give, what not to give, how to give it, and the blessing you'd get for giving.

70 First Corinthians gave guidelines for giving that created a balance between those who had too much and those who didn't have enough.

71 The New Testament commanded people not to be slothful or conceited, and not to be drunk or hang out with bad people.

72 The Apostle Paul taught that gossip is bad behavior. His letters to the Ephesians encouraged them to act more like Jesus.

73 The New Testament commanded that one "do all things without complaint."

74 The Epistle of 2 Thessalonians directed people to comfort the weak and feebleminded.

75 The Apostle Timothy charged the rich not to be conceited about their positions, and to do good work for people who are less fortunate.

The Code of Hammurabi, inscribed in stone, about 1750 B.C.E.

25 PAINFUL FACTS ABOUT

1

Crucifixion

WAS MEANT TO SHAME THE VICTIM. SOLDIERS TIED OR NAILED THE CONDEMNED TO A CROSS. AFTER A WEEK OR SO, THE PERSON DIED IN AGONY.

2

To execute by **stoning,** a prisoner was likely put in a pit, and then a group threw stones. No one knew who threw the killing blow; ALL WERE RESPONSIBLE.

3

FLOGGING

WAS A PUNISHMENT IN WHICH A PRISONER WAS BEATEN WITH RODS, BRANCHES, OR WHIPS THAT MIGHT HAVE SEVERAL STRAPS, LATER CALLED "cat-o'-nine-tails."

4

SCOURGING BY THE ROMANS WAS EXTREME FLOGGING, USING WHIPS WITH METAL OR BONE TIPS. PEOPLE OFTEN DIED FROM BLOOD LOSS. JESUS WAS SCOURGED, THEN CRUCIFIED.

5

PAUL WROTE ABOUT THE SECOND COMING OF JESUS, DESCRIBING JESUS AND MIGHTY ANGELS IN FLAMING FIRE, READY TO PUNISH THOSE WHO DID NOT FOLLOW THE GOSPEL.

6

King Belshazzar drank from GOBLETS TAKEN FROM THE TEMPLE and praised pagan gods. God warned that he was doomed; THE KING WAS KILLED IN HIS SLEEP.

7

When **KING HEROD AGRIPPA** allowed his supporters to claim he was a god, God had an angel strike Herod down, **AND HE WAS EATEN ALIVE BY WORMS.**

8

Angels helped LOT AND HIS WIFE escape Sodom, an evil city God would destroy, and told Lot not to look back. HIS WIFE DID, AND BECAME A PILLAR OF SALT.

9

WHEN MOVING THE ARK OF THE COVENANT IN AN OXCART, UZZAH STEADIED THE ARK WHEN THE OX STUMBLED. BECAUSE HE TOUCHED THE HOLY OBJECT, GOD STRUCK HIM DEAD.

10

IN REVELATION, **LOCUSTS** WITH HUMAN FACES, LIONS' TEETH, IRON SCALES, AND STINGING TAILS TORTURED THOSE WHO DID NOT WEAR GOD'S SEAL ON THEIR FOREHEAD.

11

INFURIATED BY THE SINNERS IN JERUSALEM, GOD THREATENED TO BLOW A FIERY WIND SO HOT THAT PEOPLE WOULD MELT LIKE METAL.

12

WHEN THE EGYPTIAN PHARAOH ENSLAVED THE ISRAELITES, HE OPPRESSED THEM, WEIGHING THEM DOWN WITH HARD LABOR.

13

UNHAPPY WITH EARTH'S SINFULNESS, GOD SENT RAIN FOR 40 DAYS AND 40 NIGHTS, FLOODING IT AND DESTROYING LIFE. ONLY THOSE HE SENT ONTO NOAH'S ARK LIVED.

PUNISHMENTS

14

WHEN MOSES FOUND HIS PEOPLE WORSHIPPING A GOLDEN CALF, HE GROUND IT INTO POWDER, MIXED THE GRAINS WITH WATER, AND FORCED THEM TO DRINK IT.

15

THE DEATH PENALTY was given for murder, AND ALSO FOR PICKING UP sticks on the Sabbath, WITCHCRAFT, TAKING God's name in vain, OR CURSING YOUR PARENTS.

16

As punishment for tempting Eve in the Garden of Eden, **the snake was condemned to crawl on its belly and eat dust** for all the days of its life.

17

THE ISRAELITES WERE TOLD NOT TO TAKE SPOILS FROM THE BATTLE OF JERICHO. WHEN ACHAN HID GOLD, SILVER, AND A CLOAK UNDER HIS TENT, **he was stoned to death.**

18

Early church members sold property and gave all proceeds to the church. ANANIAS AND HIS WIFE KEPT SOME PROCEEDS AND LIED ABOUT IT. They dropped **DEAD.**

19

Abimelech wanted to be king, so he killed his competitors, his 70 brothers. God had a woman drop a **millstone** on his head, crushing it.

20

When **Elisha** cured a leader of leprosy, he told his servant, Gehazi, to refuse reward. Gehazi asked for silver and clothes, so **HE GOT LEPROSY.**

21

A PRISONER OF WAR MIGHT HAVE HIS TONGUE CUT OUT OR HIS RIGHT EYE STABBED SO THAT HE COULD NO LONGER AIM ACCURATELY AT HIS TARGET WITH HIS ARROW.

22

An eye for an eye, tooth for tooth, hand for hand, foot for foot, was a rule of fairness, so that a punishment was equal to, not worse than, a crime.

23

The Philistines captured the Israelites' Ark of the Covenant. Wherever they took it, residents got tumors—a sign of God's anger with the Philistines.

24

KING ADONI-BEZEK CUT OFF THE THUMBS AND BIG TOES OF PRISONERS OF WAR SO THEY COULDN'T RUN OR USE WEAPONS. HE GOT THIS SAME TREATMENT WHEN HE WAS CAPTURED.

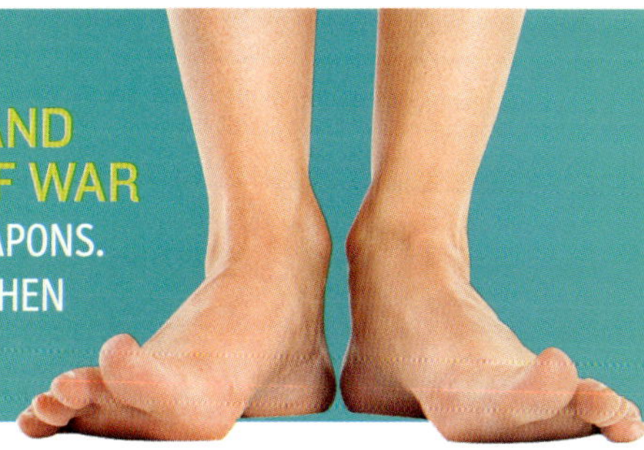

25

ACCORDING TO REVELATION, AT THE END OF THE WORLD GOD WILL PUNISH SINNERS WHO DO NOT REPENT **BY THROWING THEM INTO A LAKE OF FIRE.**

15 TRENDY FACTS ABOUT

❶ After God destroyed Israel because of the people's wicked ways, Micah was so sad for them **that he stopped wearing sandals and went barefoot.**

❷ **It was important to dress in your best clothes for a wedding.** If you forgot to wear your wedding robe you might be questioned by the king.

❸ In biblical times, **men wore a knee-length tunic,** like a long shirt, belted with a sash of linen or leather. Over this they might wear either a cloak, like a cape, or a coat, like a bathrobe.

❹ Tunics could be squares of cloth, **tied at the shoulder, or wrapped around the body.**

❺ **Women wore long tunics that covered their feet.** Their sashes were wider than men's, and decorated with colored threads and fringes nearly touching the floor.

❻ Deuteronomy stated that it was **illegal to make a garment mixing wool and linen.**

❼ The Israelites wore **blue tassels** on the four corners of their tunics to remind them not to break the commandments. **The blue dye came from sea snails.**

❽ **Cloaks were highly valued and expensive.** If you took someone's cloak as a guarantee that they'd pay back a loan, **it was law to return it by sundown, even if you had not been paid back.**

Richly colored, sequined fabrics on display in the Grand Bazaar in Istanbul, Turkey

CLOTHING TO TRY ON

❾ After they disobeyed God by eating the forbidden fruit, Adam and Eve realized they were naked. They sewed fig leaves together to cover themselves.

❿ High priests wore gem-encrusted vests embroidered with colorful yarn, and turbans with pure gold plates engraved with the words "Holy to the Lord."

⓫ Joseph's brothers were very jealous when their father gave him a beautiful coat.

⓬ Unmarried women may have covered their faces with a veil out of modesty. Rebekah did this when she first saw her future husband, Isaac, coming toward her.

⓭ The poor wore sackcloth made from goat and camel hair. Royals and the wealthy wore garments made from silk and linen. Everyone else wore wool and cotton.

⓮ Only the wealthy wore shoes; most people wore sandals. To keep the sandals from wearing out, people went barefoot on journeys, then put them on at their destination.

⓯ Beautifully embroidered garments indicated status, which meant the individual wearing it was wealthy and powerful.

15 LONG AND SHORT

❶ When Isaac's first son was born, he looked as if he were covered by a **red hairy blanket.** Isaac named him **Esau, which means "hairy"** in Hebrew.

❷ Before God called him to be a prophet, **Elijah** was a wild and woolly man **living in a cave and wearing clothes made from camel hair.**

❸ **Samson's strength came from his hair.** Delilah betrayed him by having his head shaved while Samson slept, robbing him of his supernatural strength.

❹ **Absalom only got his hair cut once a year.** The pile of shorn locks was so big it weighed 200 shekels—**about five pounds (2.2 kg).**

❺ After God took away the vain King Nebuchadnezzar's kingdom and made him an outcast, **the king's hair grew like eagle feathers and his nails like bird claws.**

❻ The Book of Numbers defined a **Nazirite** as a holy person who vowed to God not to drink wine and to **"let the locks of the head grow long."**

❼ The priest and scribe **Ezra was so upset** when he heard that Israelites were marrying their enemies the Egyptians that **he plucked out his hair and beard.**

Detail from fresco of Samson at Altlerchenfelder Church, Vienna, Austria

FACTS ABOUT HAIR

8. When **Job** discovered that all his children, servants, and animals had died during God's test of his faith, **he tore his clothes and shaved his head.**

9. In Ezekiel, people were told to **use their swords to shave their heads and beards.** Then they were to divide the hair into thirds: a third to burn after the siege of Jerusalem, a third to strike with the sword, **and the rest to scatter in the wind.**

10. According to Matthew, God knows you so well that **he knows every strand of hair on your head.**

11. According to the New Testament, it's disgraceful for men to have long hair, **but long hair is a woman's glory.**

12. King Solomon's poem, the Song of Solomon, praises a bride's beauty: **"Your hair is like a flock of goats moving down the slopes of [Mount] Gilead."**

13. While **Absalom** was riding his mule, **his long locks got tangled in the branches of an oak tree.** His mule kept going, leaving Absalom swinging in midair, an easy target for enemy spears.

14. To make themselves clean in God's eyes, **some men would shave all their hair,** including their beards and **the tops of their feet.**

15. At a dinner given in Jesus' honor, his follower Mary (not his mother) **rubbed perfume on Jesus' feet, then wiped his feet with her hair.**

15 FACTS ABOUT WEAPONS

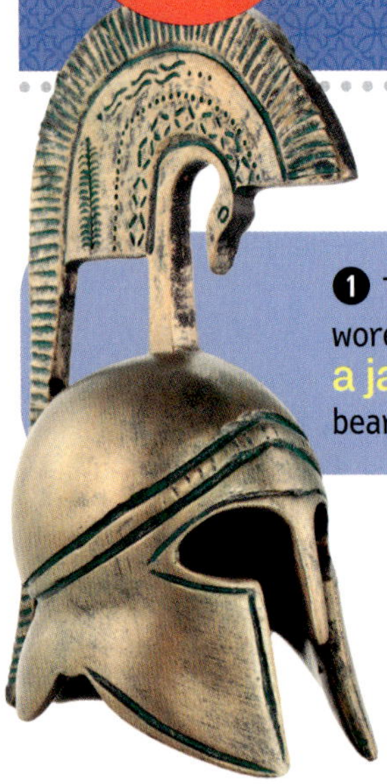

❶ To fight David, the giant **Goliath** wore a bronze helmet and armor and carried **a javelin, spear, and sword.** A shield bearer walked before him.

❷ When Isaiah prophesied that **swords would be turned into plowshares**—plow blades for farming—he meant there would someday be peace in the world.

❸ After Adam and Eve left the Garden of Eden, an **angel wielding a flaming sword** guarded the entrance.

❹ Armed with only a **slingshot and stones,** David defeated Goliath with **one well-aimed shot** that sunk into his forehead.

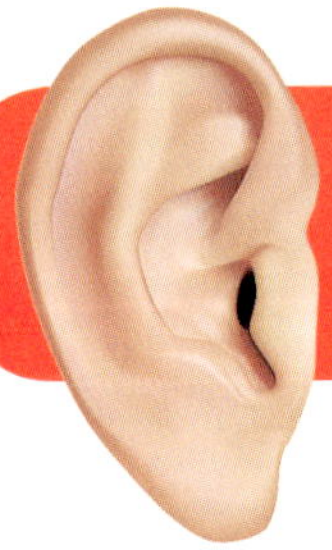

❺ To try to stop the arrest of Jesus in the Garden of Gethsemane, **Peter drew his sword and cut off the ear** of a servant of the high priest.

❻ **The Book of Hebrews** compares the word of God to **a sharp, two-edged sword** that can penetrate a person's soul and judge his thoughts.

❼ As **David played the lyre for King Saul,** the king was overcome with jealousy for the boy's talents and **hurled a spear at David.** David escaped.

❽ **War chariots** helped armies charge into battle. The Canaanite leader Sisera commanded **900 iron chariots** in battles against the Israelites.

THAT WILL HAVE YOU UP IN ARMS

A stone relief from the palace of Ashurbanipal at Nineveh

❾ The weapons mentioned most often in the Bible are among the simplest: the sword and the dagger.

❿ Warhorses may have been the deadliest "weapon" in battle, killing more enemies than arrows. How? When soldiers fell, they were often crushed under the hooves.

⓫ The first weapon used by a human in the Bible is an ordinary rock. Cain used it to kill his brother Abel.

⓬ Weapons were used for hunting as well as fighting. The bow and arrow is first mentioned in Genesis as a tool for hunting game.

⓭ The Book of Psalms says to put faith in God, not weapons: "For not in my bow do I trust, nor can my sword save me. But you have saved me from our foes."

⓮ Shepherds carried weapons to protect themselves from wild animals—usually stones, staffs, and slingshots.

⓯ The Book of Ecclesiastes warns against putting too much faith in swords and shields and bows and arrows. It says that wisdom is better than weapons.

25 FIGHTING FACTS

1

During the BATTLE OF JERICHO, the Israelites marched around the city blowing horns AND THE CITY WALL FELL DOWN.

2

Instead of the full Israelite army fighting the full Philistine army, only two men, one from each side, faced each other: David and Goliath.

3

WHEN GOING INTO BATTLE, THE ISRAELITES BELIEVED GOD FOUGHT WITH THEM AGAINST THEIR ENEMIES.

4

Many battles were sieges—when an army surrounds a city and bombards and starves it until it surrenders. Joshua and his army did this to the city of Lachish.

5

The Book of Deuteronomy told military leaders to offer a town "TERMS OF PEACE" before they attacked it.

6

BABYLON'S KING NEBUCHADNEZZAR CONQUERED JERUSALEM AND SENT ITS PEOPLE INTO EXILE, INCLUDING "ALL THE MEN OF VALOR, (WHO TOTALED) SEVEN THOUSAND."

7

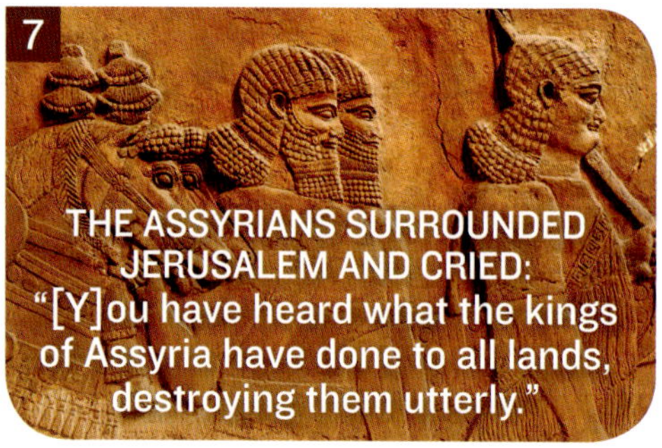

THE ASSYRIANS SURROUNDED JERUSALEM AND CRIED: "[Y]ou have heard what the kings of Assyria have done to all lands, destroying them utterly."

8

THE BOOK OF PSALMS WARNS AGAINST NATIONS THAT "DELIGHT IN WAR."

9

ACCORDING TO DEUTERONOMY, males 20 years and older could be made to join the army. Men married less than a year did not have to join.

10

Just like today, armies used SPIES to find out what the enemy was up to before a battle started.

11

THE ISRAELITES OFTEN BLEW TRUMPETS OF RAMS' HORNS, OR SHOFARS, BEFORE A BATTLE. THIS PROBABLY SCARED THE ENEMY BEFORE THE FIGHTING STARTED.

12

Winning armies often took THE SPOILS, or possessions, of the losers, SUCH AS MONEY, CATTLE, AND WEAPONS, unless commanded not to.

13

SOMETIMES GOD ORDERED THAT NOTHING BE TAKEN FROM THE LOSING CITY. A SOLDIER DISOBEYED GOD'S ORDER AT JERICHO, so the Israelites lost a later battle.

ABOUT BATTLES

14

AS LONG AS **MOSES KEPT HIS HANDS RAISED IN BATTLE** WITH THE AMALEKITES, **THE ISRAELITES WON.** AARON AND HUR HELPED HOLD UP HIS HANDS ALL DAY.

15

The **BOOK OF ISAIAH** prophesied, or predicted, a time when battles and **warfare will come to an END.**

16

One of the **FINAL GREAT BATTLES** in the New Testament's Book of Revelation is **ARMAGEDDON,** a struggle between **GOOD AND EVIL** at the end of the world.

17

In Chronicles, the Israelites beat **three enemies at once:** God made the enemies fight among themselves and **"destroy one another."**

18

Gideon had a powerful army of Israelites to defeat the Midianites, but God told him to use only **300 men** so Gideon would know that God let him win.

19

THE BATTLE AGAINST THE KING OF BASHAN WAS WON BEFORE IT STARTED. GOD TOLD MOSES, **"Do not be afraid of him; for I have given him into your hand."**

20

When the **Arameans** besieged the Israelites in Samaria, **GOD CAUSED THE ATTACKERS TO HEAR A MASSIVE ARMY APPROACHING.** The Arameans ran.

21

In his battles against the Philistines, Samson was like a one-man army. In one fight, **he killed a thousand men with the jawbone of a donkey.**

22

When the Israelites were defeated by the Philistines at Ebenezer, THEY LOST **30,000** MEN AND THE ARK OF THE COVENANT HOLDING **THE TEN COMMANDMENTS.**

23

After losing to the Philistines, King Saul **decided to kill himself rather than be taken prisoner—** "So Saul took his own sword and fell on it."

24

IN DEUTERONOMY, **THE ISRAELITES IGNORED GOD'S COMMAND NOT TO ATTACK THE AMORITES,** AND THE ISRAELITES **LOST THE BATTLE.**

25

WHEN THE ASSYRIANS SURROUNDED JERUSALEM, GOD SAID HE WOULD SAVE THE CITY AND SENT **AN ANGEL** WHO **KILLED 185,000** ASSYRIAN SOLDIERS.

25 BLOOMING FACTS ABOUT PLANTS

1 Because of DIFFERENT LANDSCAPES, elevations, and soils, from lush river valleys to deserts, biblical Israel had a VARIETY OF PLANTS AND FLOWERS.

2 

The forbidden fruit in the Garden of Eden is often thought to be an apple. The Bible doesn't say. Some think it was an apricot, or a pomegranate.

3 

THERE WERE **FIG TREES** IN THE GARDEN OF EDEN. ADAM AND EVE COVERED THEMSELVES WITH FIG LEAVES AFTER REALIZING THEY WERE NAKED.

4 PLANTS WERE THE MAIN SOURCE OF REMEDIES FOR HEALING. IN THE BOOK OF ISAIAH, THE PROPHET SUGGESTS **treating a boil by putting figs on it.**

5 Plants and flowers were among the things God created on the **third day in Genesis** and "saw that it was good."

6 **Frankincense and myrrh** were brought by the **WISE MEN** to young Jesus. These fragrant, gumlike substances came from trees on the Arabian Peninsula.

7 LEBANON'S **CEDAR FORESTS** PROVIDED MUCH OF THE WOOD THE ISRAELITES USED FOR CONSTRUCTION. DAVID USED IT TO BUILD HIS PALACE AND SOLOMON HIS TEMPLE.

8 Jesus said that not even King Solomon in all his glory could match the beauty of the **lilies of the field.**

9 

WHEN **JESUS** MADE HIS TRIUMPHAL ENTRY INTO JERUSALEM SHORTLY BEFORE HIS DEATH, THE PEOPLE HONORED HIM BY LAYING **PALM TREE BRANCHES** IN HIS PATH.

10 IN THE GOSPEL OF JOHN, Jesus described himself as THE TRUE VINE, his Father as THE GARDENER, and his followers as **THE BRANCHES.**

11 SOME PEOPLE BELIEVE THAT WHILE ADAM AND EVE WERE STILL IN THE GARDEN OF EDEN THEY WERE **VEGETARIANS** WHO ATE NO MEAT, ONLY PLANTS.

12 **ACACIA WOOD** was used to build the Ark of the Covenant and other sacred objects. The tree's deep roots easily reach water beneath the dry desert.

13 After the Israelites left Egypt and crossed the desert, they came to a fruitful valley called Elim that had **12 springs of water and 70 palm trees.**

14 GOD TOLD THE ISRAELITES THAT **THE PROMISED LAND** WAS A LAND OF "WHEAT AND BARLEY AND VINES AND FIG TREES, AND POMEGRANATES, . . . OLIVE TREES AND HONEY."

15 As gifts for the governor of Egypt, Jacob's sons took HONEY, PISTACHIO NUTS, ALMONDS, SPICES, AND MYRRH.

16 In the Book of Revelation, **THE TREE OF LIFE** had 12 kinds of fruit, with new fruit each month; its leaves were for "the healing of the nations."

17 **GOD TOLD DAVID** HE WOULD GO BEFORE HIM AND HIS ARMY TO STRIKE DOWN THE PHILISTINES, BUT NOT UNTIL DAVID HEARD **A STIRRING IN THE BALSAM TREES.**

AND FLOWERS

18 WHEN EGYPT'S PHARAOH WANTED TO KILL HEBREW BABY BOYS, MOSES' MOTHER HID HIM ON THE NILE RIVERBANK IN A BASKET WOVEN OF **PAPYRUS,** A WATER PLANT.

19

For their first **Passover meal** in Egypt, the Israelites ate meat "with bitter herbs" and bread made of wheat, but without yeast.

20 **Hyssop,** a plant in the mint family, was used to purify and cleanse houses and temples.

21 While wandering in the desert, the Israelites wished for the food they had eaten in Egypt: fish, cucumbers, melons, leeks, onions, and garlic.

22 THE ROMAN SOLDIERS PLACED **A CROWN OF THORNS** ON JESUS' HEAD, AND LAUGHED AT THE IDEA THAT JESUS COULD BE A KING.

23 After **Jonah** escaped the big fish and took God's message to the people of Nineveh, he rested under a bush God grew to give him shade.

24 WHEN **KING DAVID** ESCAPED FROM HIS SON ABSALOM, WHO WAS TRYING TO KILL HIM, HIS SUPPORTERS GAVE HIM **BEANS, LENTILS, BARLEY, AND OTHER FOOD.**

25 GOD TOLD MOSES TO MAKE A SACRED ANOINTING OIL USING **CINNAMON** AND OTHER FINE SPICES.

1
The Bible opens with an act of God—God's **creation of the universe.**

2
According to modern U.S. law, an **"act of God"** today is a term for a natural disaster, like a hurricane, or any event beyond human control.

3
Tired of humans disobeying him, **God sent a great flood** to wash them away. He saved Noah and his family, who floated in an ark God told Noah to build.

4
When the people grew too powerful and tried to build a tower to heaven, God confused them by making them all **speak different languages.**

5
At Solomon's Temple, the sick were laid outside on cots. When the Apostle Peter walked by, **his shadow fell on them and they were cured.**

6
When the pharaoh refused to let the Israelites leave Egypt, **God sent ten plagues** to change his mind, including turning the rivers into blood.

7
To help the Israelites escape the Egyptians, **God parted the Red Sea** so they could cross on dry land; then he closed it, drowning the Egyptians.

8
As Joshua was winning a battle against the Amorites, the sun began to set. **God stopped the sun** and extended the day so Joshua could end the battle.

9
When the Prophet Elijah went to heaven, he traveled in a **chariot of fire.**

10
The king of Persia threw Daniel into a den of lions for disobeying an order not to pray to God. God sent an angel **to shut the lions' mouths,** and Daniel lived.

11
Enoch was Noah's great-grandfather. Like the Prophet Elijah, **Enoch may never have died.** The Bible simply says that God took them.

12
Three young Jews refused to worship a gold statue set up by Babylon's King Nebuchadnezzar. He threw them into a fiery furnace, **and they were unhurt.**

13
Jonah boarded a ship to run away from God's command. When Jonah was thrown overboard in a storm, **God sent a great fish** to rescue him.

14
God wrote on wicked King Belshazzar's wall that **his end was near.**

15
In Exodus, God caught Moses' attention with **a burning bush:** It was covered in flames but did not actually burn up.

16
Moses carried an amazing wooden staff as he led the Israelites from Egypt. It could **produce water from a rock** and could turn into a snake and back again.

17
When you hear **"that's manna from heaven,"** it means there's a welcome surprise. Manna was food God sent the hungry Israelites after they left Egypt.

18
Naaman, a mighty commander of the Syrian army, had leprosy. The Prophet **Elisha cured it** by having Naaman **bathe seven times in the Jordan River.**

19
In the New Testament, God's son, Jesus, took on a human body and became both God and man. This miracle is called **the Incarnation.**

20
To lead the wise men to the newborn Jesus, **God placed a star in the heavens** that they followed from their homes to Jerusalem.

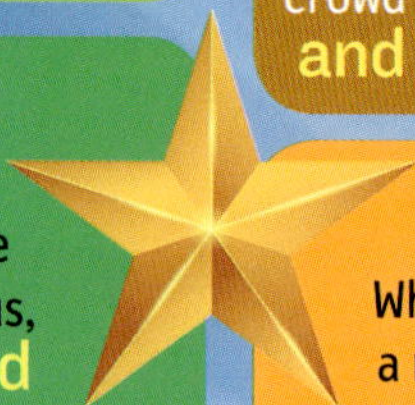

21
Jesus' first miracle came at a wedding. When the host ran out of wine for his guests, **Jesus turned water into wine.**

22
When his disciples were having no luck catching fish, Jesus told them to **cast their nets again.** They caught so many fish, their boats nearly sank!

23
To cure a man suffering from leprosy, Jesus simply **touched** him.

24
Frightened during a storm on the Sea of Galilee, the disciples woke Jesus as he slept in the back of the boat. With a command, he **calmed the sea.**

25
Jesus met a man possessed by many **demons.** Jesus sent the demons into a herd of pigs that ran into a lake and drowned.

26
Sometimes Jesus seemed to perform miracles without even trying, as when a bleeding woman in a crowd **touched him and was healed.**

27
When Jesus healed a mute—someone who could not talk—the **Pharisees,** or religious rulers, said he had healing powers because he was the **prince of demons.**

28
Jesus told a man who was lame, or disabled, to **get up and walk**—he did!

29
Just how far can **five loaves and two fish** go? In one Gospel, Jesus turned them into enough food to feed at least **5,000 people.**

50 Facts About MIRACLES

30
During a Sea of Galilee storm, the disciples saw Jesus **walking to them on the water.** Peter crawled from the boat to walk, too, but sank.

31
To pay taxes, most people have to get money from the bank. **Jesus pulled a coin from the mouth of a fish** to pay his temple tax, and Peter's, too.

32
One time, Jesus healed ten men from **leprosy.** Only one thanked him.

33
Jesus' miracles and healings made the Pharisees angry, especially when he carried them out on the Jewish holy day, **the Sabbath.**

34
Lazarus had been dead for four days by the time Jesus arrived to heal him. Jesus healed him anyway—**by raising him from the dead.**

35
Jesus returned eyesight to Bartimaeus, a blind man from Jericho.

36
Peter defended Jesus by **cutting off the ear** of the high priest's servant in the Garden of Gethsemane. Jesus touched the man's ear and **healed him.**

37
One of Jesus' miracles was **exorcism,** or driving out evil spirits.

38
Three days after Jesus died, **he came back to life.**

39
John's Gospel says that the New Testament tells only some of Jesus' miracles. **All his miracles would fill more books than the world could hold.**

40
God destroyed the evil cities Sodom and Gomorrah by raining down **sulfur.**

41
On the journey from Egypt, the Israelites complained that the water at Marah was **bitter.** Moses threw a piece of wood into it and **it turned sweet.**

42
As the Israelites gathered at the foot of Mount Sinai, God descended upon the top in fire, and the whole **mountain trembled** violently.

43
To lead the Israelites through the desert by day, **God appeared as a pillar of cloud.** At night, he appeared as **a pillar of fire.**

44
To save the Prophet Elijah from King Ahab, God told him to flee to a brook called Cherith. There, **ravens brought Elijah bread and meat** twice a day.

45
When Ahab's son Ahaziah sent a captain and 50 men to capture Elijah, the prophet called down **fire from heaven** and killed them.

46
Rebuked by a prophet, **Jeroboam** stretched out his hand and ordered the prophet's arrest. **His hand withered** before his eyes.

47
Before **Elijah** rose to heaven, he dropped his cloak by the Jordan River. Elisha picked it up, hit the river with it, and **the waters parted;** he walked across.

48
Joshua **halted the Jordan River's flow** so the Ark of the Covenant could be taken across.

49
The angel **Gabriel** told Mary, "You have found favor with God. You will conceive and give birth to a son, and you are to call him **Jesus.**"

50
When Jesus finally left the disciples, **"he was lifted up and ... out of their sight."**

25 TEMPLES AND TEMPLE

1 AFTER LEAVING EGYPT, THE ISRAELITES WORSHIPPED IN **A MOVABLE TENT** CALLED THE TABERNACLE OR **TENT OF MEETING.** GOD TOLD THEM HOW TO CREATE AND FURNISH IT.

2 The tent's outer court held the **ALTAR OF BURNT OFFERING** for burning sacrifices, and a bronze basin where priests washed before entering.

3 To summon all the people, **Moses blew two trumpets** made from hammered silver.

4 The tent's **HOLY PLACE** held the lampstand, the altar of incense, and the table of the bread of the Presence with 12 loaves of bread for Israel's 12 tribes.

5 ARCHAEOLOGISTS FOUND A **STONE ALTAR AT SHILOH,** WHERE THE TENT LIKELY WAS BUILT. ON IT, THE ISRAELITES MAY HAVE MADE THEIR FIRST OFFERINGS INSIDE ISRAEL.

6 THE SEVEN-BRANCHED **LAMPSTAND** WAS PERHAPS FIVE FEET (1.5 M) HIGH AND FUELED WITH OLIVE OIL. PRIESTS KEPT THE LAMPS BURNING "FROM EVENING TO MORNING."

7 Moses mixed an **incense recipe of spices and frankincense** only for use in temples and on altars. Its scented smoke rose from the altar of incense.

8 THE INNERMOST ROOM OF THE TENT, THE HOLY OF HOLIES, CONTAINED ONLY ONE PIECE— **THE ARK OF THE COVENANT.**

9 THE ARK, a wooden, gold-plated chest, held THE TEN COMMANDMENTS, A POT OF MANNA, AND THE ROD OF MOSES' BROTHER, AARON, symbolizing his leadership.

10 **The Arch of Titus** in Rome has carvings of Jerusalem's Holy Temple being robbed by the Romans in 70 C.E. One image shows soldiers taking the lampstand.

11 THE PURE-GOLD LID OF THE ARK OF THE COVENANT WAS CALLED **THE MERCY SEAT.** ON IT, TWO PURE-GOLD CHERUBS FACED ONE ANOTHER WITH THEIR WINGS SPREAD.

12 Temples were places of **WORSHIP.** Anyone could gather or pray in an outer area enclosed by columns. Only priests could go into the inner chambers.

ARTIFACT FACTS

13

A LINEN VEIL divided the temple's Holy Place from the Holy of Holies. The Gospel of Matthew says that **WHEN JESUS DIED, THIS VEIL WAS TORN IN TWO.**

14

SOLOMON'S TEMPLE WAS ISRAEL'S FIRST MAJOR TEMPLE. GOD DID NOT LET SOLOMON'S FATHER, DAVID, BUILD IT BECAUSE HE WAS A WARRIOR, SO SOLOMON BUILT IT.

15

SYNAGOGUE is Greek for "a gathering of people." Like a temple, it is a place for worship, but less formal. Jesus' first teachings were in synagogues.

16

The Babylonians destroyed Solomon's Temple and enslaved the Israelites. About 516 B.C.E., they were freed. Zerubbabel began building Israel's second temple.

17

WHEN SOLOMON'S SON, **REHOBOAM,** RULED IN THE TENTH CENTURY B.C.E., EGYPT'S PHARAOH ATTACKED JERUSALEM, TAKING TEMPLE TREASURES LIKE SOLOMON'S GOLD SHIELDS.

18

HEROD doubled the size of ZERUBBABEL'S TEMPLE. He used marble and gold, and put a retaining wall around it. Some call it **ISRAEL'S THIRD MAJOR TEMPLE.**

19

THE PUBLIC ENTRANCE TO THE COURTYARD OF HEROD'S TEMPLE WAS CALLED THE **BEAUTIFUL GATE.** HERE THE APOSTLE PETER HEALED A BEGGAR WHO COULD NOT WALK.

20

Only the Western Wall of Herod's Temple remains. Once called the **WAILING WALL,** where Jews wept about the temple's ruin, today it is a place of prayer.

21

At Tell Ta'yinat and 'Ain Dara, in Turkey and Syria, ARCHAEOLOGISTS HAVE UNCOVERED TEMPLES RESEMBLING SOLOMON'S TEMPLE AS IT WAS DESCRIBED IN THE BIBLE.

22

Temples were more than places for worship. In ancient times, they were often centers of knowledge, money, and political power.

23

During digs at Khirbet Qeiyafa, near Jerusalem, archaeologists found **stone shrines shaped like temples,** built 30 to 40 years before King David's time.

24

ANCIENT SCROLLS, roughly dated from Zerubbabel's era, were found in caves near the Dead Sea. **One held plans for a new temple to be built in Jerusalem.**

25

TO BUILD SOLOMON'S TEMPLE, workers used CEDAR WOOD, PRECIOUS METALS, AND STONES CUT FROM A QUARRY, or stone pit, and hauled to the site.

75 HARD-WORKING

❶ Hiram, king of Tyre, sent carpenters and stonemasons to help build King David's palace in Jerusalem.

❷ Mary's husband, Joseph, was a *tektonos*, Greek for "carpenter" or "craftsman." Jesus was first known as "the carpenter's son."

❸ At the time of Jesus' birth during the reign of Caesar Augustus, census takers registered all the inhabitants of Israel.

❹ A shepherd's job was often around-the-clock. When Jesus was born, shepherds were guarding their flocks by night.

❺ MOSES WAS A PRINCE OF EGYPT AND LATER THE LEADER OF THE ISRAELITES. IN BETWEEN, HE WAS A SHEPHERD WHO TENDED THE FLOCKS OF HIS FATHER-IN-LAW.

❻ The Book of Genesis defines cattlemen as "those who live in tents and have livestock."

❼ Tubal-Cain, a descendant of Adam and Eve's son Cain, was a tinsmith, one "who made . . . bronze and iron tools."

❽ Jesus visited Zacchaeus, a wealthy Jericho tax collector, who said that if he'd cheated anyone, he would "pay back four times as much."

❾ In the King James Bible, the tax collectors of the New Testament are called "publicans." The Latin *publicanus* means "of the people."

❿ During Jesus' time, tax collectors were disliked. Many people thought they worked for Rome, the unwelcome foreign occupier.

⓫ When Jesus first met him, the future Apostle Matthew was a tax collector sitting in his booth.

⓬ THE APOSTLE PAUL WROTE OF A COPPERSMITH NAMED ALEXANDER "WHO DID HIM GREAT HARM." WE DON'T KNOW HOW.

⓭ In Genesis, a baker dreamed that birds were eating the food he'd baked for Pharaoh; Pharaoh later threw him into prison.

⓮ Nehemiah was a cupbearer for the king of Persia. He tasted each drink before the king did, in case it was poisoned.

⓯ The Prophet Samuel's cook served King Saul a special cut of meat when the king was Samuel's guest.

⓰ The Book of Matthew mentions the grinders, who turned grain into flour for bread.

⓱ Peter and his brother Andrew were fishermen on the Sea of Galilee. Jesus offered them jobs as "fishers of men," or missionaries.

⓲ GENESIS IDENTIFIES JUBAL, A DESCENDANT OF CAIN, AS THE FATHER OF "ALL WHO HANDLE THE HARP AND THE ORGAN."

⓳ Isaac's wife, Rebekah, had a nurse named Deborah, who stayed with the family until she died.

⓴ Nimrod, a descendant of Noah, was the first hunter mentioned in the Bible, called "a mighty hunter before the Lord."

㉑ Adam and Eve's firstborn, Cain, was a farmer, "a tiller of the ground."

㉒ The younger brother of Cain, Abel was "a keeper of sheep."

㉓ Judges ruled over Israel before the nation had kings.

㉔ The judges appointed Saul the first king of Israel. God told the judge and prophet Samuel: "[H]e will govern my people."

㉕ SECOND ONLY TO THE PHARAOH, JOSEPH BECAME THE GOVERNOR OF EGYPT, THE PERSON "WHO SOLD [GRAIN] TO ALL THE PEOPLE OF THE LAND."

㉖ Daniel became one of 120 governors, called *satraps* in ancient Persian, who ruled regions of the Median Empire.

㉗ In Roman Palestine, a jailer had to keep his prisoners from escaping. If they escaped, he was jailed in their place, and for their term.

㉘ Scribes kept written records, and copied and interpreted Moses' law from God. The scribe Ezra studied and taught the law in Israel.

㉙ The Bible describes Jehoshaphat as a recorder in King Solomon's court. He kept a record of daily events.

㉚ The brothers Elihoreph and Ahijah were two of King Solomon's "high officials"—or secretaries.

㉛ Solomon had 12 district governors. Each one supplied goods to the king's household for one month of the year.

㉜ AFTER JOSHUA WAS DECEIVED BY THE GIBEONITES, HE PUNISHED THEM BY GIVING THEM LOWLY JOBS, SUCH AS WOODCUTTERS AND WATER CARRIERS.

㉝ A goldsmith, a perfumer, and other workers came together to rebuild Jerusalem's walls after a fire destroyed them.

㉞ Paul's teaching about God in the city of Ephesus worried the silversmiths, who made silver shrines for the goddess Artemis.

㉟ With no blacksmiths in Israel, the Israelites went to the Philistines to sharpen their plow points, mattocks, axes, and sickles.

Fishing nets used by fishermen

FACTS ABOUT JOBS

36 The Bible compares God to a potter who has the right to make out of the same lump of clay some pottery for special purposes and some for common use.

37 In the port of Joppa, Peter stayed with a tanner named Simon. A tanner turns animal skins into leather.

38 The Apostle Paul was a tentmaker.

39 THE BOOK OF MALACHI MENTIONS A FULLER—A LAUNDERER OR CLEANER OF FABRIC.

40 A good Samaritan helped a man who'd been attacked by robbers, then paid an innkeeper two denarii to care for him.

41 Chronicles describes the descendants of Issachar as "mighty warriors" who numbered 87,000.

42 In Isaiah, God explains that he made David "a leader and commander for the people."

43 In Psalms, a procession into God's sanctuary included singers, musicians, and young women playing timbrels, or tambourines.

44 IN BIBLICAL TIMES, THE KING WAS NOT JUST THE POLITICAL RULER, BUT ALSO AN EXAMPLE OF WISDOM TO HIS PEOPLE.

45 The Book of Acts calls Sergius Paulus, a Roman official who helped govern the provinces, "an intelligent man."

46 According to Genesis, Noah planted the first vineyard. Vinedressers were workers who kept up the vineyards.

47 Merchants often paid by barter, exchanging goods for other goods rather than using money.

48 Twelve thousand horsemen took care of the 1,400 chariots in King Solomon's army.

49 The treasurer for Candace, Queen of the Ethiopians, was in charge of the queen's money.

50 THE GOSPEL WRITER LUKE WAS A GREEK DOCTOR WHO LIVED IN THE CITY OF ANTIOCH. HE WAS CALLED "OUR BELOVED PHYSICIAN."

51 In the Garden of Gethsemane, Jesus was arrested by a group of Roman soldiers and local religious officials.

52 David entered King Saul's service as an armor-bearer.

53 Caiaphas was the high priest at the time of the arrest and Crucifixion of Jesus.

54 In the Book of Leviticus, rules for priests included that they could not shave their heads or touch a dead person.

55 A watchman's job was to blow a trumpet to warn of approaching enemies. If he failed, God would hold him responsible.

56 A centurion described himself as "a man under authority, with soldiers under me."

57 One job of a prophet was to be a messenger of God.

58 AMOS MAY HAVE BEEN A PROPHET, BUT HE EARNED HIS LIVING AS A FARMER AND A HERDSMAN.

59 God instructed Aaron to ask others from his tribe to help uphold God's laws.

60 In the Book of Revelation, John said that Jesus made us all to be "priests serving his God and Father."

61 The Apostle Paul said a bishop had to be "above reproach, married only once, temperate, sensible, respectable, hospitable, an apt teacher."

62 According to Paul, Jesus gave people the gifts of becoming apostles, prophets, evangelists, pastors, and teachers.

63 In Isaiah, the cedar trees rejoiced that no tree cutter was about to chop them down.

64 When God "lays waste the earth" at the end of time, warned Isaiah, it will be the same for lenders and creditors as it is for borrowers and debtors.

65 MONEYLENDERS COULD CHARGE INTEREST TO A FOREIGNER, BUT NOT TO A FELLOW ISRAELITE.

66 Samson was a Nazirite, a holy person who usually took a special vow to God and also abstained from wine.

67 Midwives usually helped deliver babies in ancient Egypt.

68 "The laborer deserves to be paid," wrote the Apostle Paul.

69 The Prophet Isaiah mocked astrologers—"those who gaze at the stars and . . . predict what shall befall you."

70 Builders used brick and tar to build "a tower that reaches to the heavens." It would be called the Tower of Babel.

71 King Hezekiah sent Judah and messengers to plead with the people to return to the Lord.

72 TO HIDE HIS IDENTITY, JOSEPH SPOKE TO HIS BROTHERS IN THE EGYPTIAN LANGUAGE. HE USED AN INTERPRETER TO TRANSLATE HIS WORDS FOR THEM.

73 In the Book of 2 Kings, masons and stonecutters repaired the temple of the Lord.

74 While Joseph was the governor of Egypt, he employed a steward, or manager, to take care of his household.

75 The philosophers of Athens, Greece, prided themselves on their wisdom and intellect. They debated Paul about the truth of the Gospel he preached: "What does this babbler want to say?"

25 TELLING FACTS ABOUT

1 God used prophets as a way to speak to his people. They weren't always popular, because THEY OFTEN HAD TO TELL PEOPLE WHAT THEY DIDN'T WANT TO HEAR.

2 Prophets' warnings to behave **often came true,** so people thought they **PREDICTED THE FUTURE.** Prophets also advised rulers and performed symbolic acts.

3 The first person called a **PROPHET** in the Bible was **Abraham.**

4 Because the Israelites did not follow the law, GOD HAD THE PROPHET EZEKIEL **WALK AROUND NAKED** FOR THREE YEARS as a symbol of the shame God would send.

5 The Hebrew word for "prophet" is ***nabi,*** which means **"spokesman."**

6 ACCORDING TO DEUTERONOMY, **MOSES** WAS THE GREATEST OF PROPHETS, WHOM GOD KNEW FACE-TO-FACE.

7 **"In the last days,"** Peter preached, "your sons and your daughters shall **prophesy,** and your young men shall **see visions,** and your old men shall **dream dreams."**

8 **Female prophets** INCLUDED **DEBORAH,** A JUDGE AND LEADER; **MIRIAM,** MOSES' SISTER; AND **HULDAH,** ADVISER TO KING JOSIAH; AND **NOADIAH** (WHO WAS A FALSE PROPHET).

9 Prophesying about Egypt and the Nile, Isaiah foresaw a time when the **"RIVER WILL DRY UP, AND THE RIVERBED WILL BE PARCHED AND DRY."**

10 In Deuteronomy, God explained what he expected from a prophet: **"I will put my words in the mouth of the prophet, who shall speak to them everything that I command."**

11 The prophetic books of the Bible are named after the prophets who wrote them, EXCEPT FOR THE BOOK OF **JONAH,** which is written about him.

12 **Jonah** didn't want to take God's message to the WICKED PEOPLE OF NINEVEH, so he sailed in the other direction. God had him swallowed **BY A HUGE FISH.**

13 Some prophets are known as **"MAJOR PROPHETS"** and some as **"MINOR PROPHETS."** The difference was the lengths of their books.

PROPHETS

14

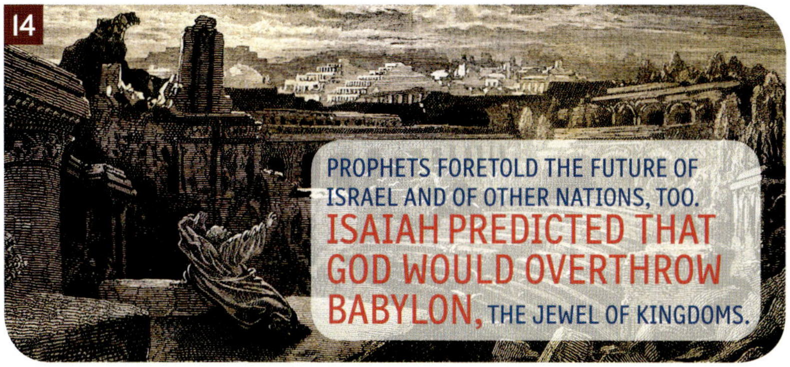

PROPHETS FORETOLD THE FUTURE OF ISRAEL AND OF OTHER NATIONS, TOO. **ISAIAH PREDICTED THAT GOD WOULD OVERTHROW BABYLON,** THE JEWEL OF KINGDOMS.

15

Prophets had varied backgrounds: **MOSES** was a prince of Egypt, **ELISHA** a plowman, and **AMOS** a herdsman. But all shared this: **THEY WERE CHOSEN BY GOD.**

16

God's messages through prophets were called **ORACLES.** They began with the words "Thus says the Lord," and warned what would happen if people didn't mend their ways.

17

After the people killed God's prophets, **Elijah** feared he would be next. **BUT HE LIVED.** AT LAST, GOD TOOK HIM TO HEAVEN, ALIVE, **IN A CHARIOT OF FIRE.**

18

IN A VISION, GOD TOOK EZEKIEL TO A VALLEY OF THE ISRAELITES' DRY BONES AND TOLD HIM TO PROPHESY THAT THEY WOULD LIVE AGAIN AND RETURN TO THEIR LAND.

19

Jeremiah, known as THE "WEEPING PROPHET," wished for a fountain of tears to weep for his people killed when the Babylonians captured Jerusalem.

20

John the Baptist WAS A **NEW TESTAMENT PROPHET.** HIS JOB WAS TO PREPARE THE PEOPLE FOR THE ARRIVAL OF **JESUS.**

21

The New Testament explains that **PROPHECIES CAME FROM GOD, NOT MEN:** "no prophecy ever came by human will, but . . . from God."

22

Many prophets had **OTHER VOCATIONS:** Deborah was a judge and **a leader of the Israelites in battle.**

23

Besides prophets, **there were false prophets** who claimed they were speaking for God but were not. **False prophets faced a punishment of DEATH.**

24

MUCH OF THE PROPHECY IN THE NEW TESTAMENT IS ABOUT **THE SECOND COMING,** WHEN **JESUS WILL RETURN TO EARTH AT THE END OF THE WORLD.**

25

SAMUEL WAS STILL A CHILD when he heard God calling him to be a prophet. He went on to anoint King Saul and King David.

15 ROUTINE FACTS

❶ Women **drew water** from city wells and **carried it home in clay jugs.** During this task, Rebekah was identified by Abraham's servant as the wife for his son Isaac.

❷ When the Israelites traveled through the desert, part of their daily routine was **eating manna,** the sacred bread that God sent to them **from heaven.**

❸ In the Book of Matthew, Jesus told a story about why every Israelite household needed to keep enough oil on hand, since **people lit their homes with oil lamps.**

❹ Always on the move with their flocks, **shepherds lived in tents.** Shepherds were watching their sheep when an angel of the Lord told them of Jesus' birth.

❺ To protect their inhabitants, cities were **surrounded by fortified walls.** The only way in or out was through one of the city gates.

❻ At harvest time, **there was no such thing as a weekend!** The Israelites lived in temporary shelters in the fields for seven days.

❼ "Take a seat" usually just meant sit on the ground. In Old Testament times, **only people in high positions actually sat on chairs.**

❽ In biblical times, **people slept on mats.** When Jesus instructed a lame man to pick up his mat and walk, he was telling him to get up and take his bed with him.

ABOUT DAILY LIFE

"The Gathering of Manna," by Francesco Bacchiacca, 1540–1555

❾ Most families had an "open door policy" to show hospitality to others—the doors to their homes were opened in the morning and stayed open all day.

❿ For building, people used bricks made of clay and baked hard in an oven, or kiln. Bricks were used to build the Tower of Babel.

⓫ In biblical times, sleeping "upstairs" might mean actually going up on the roof of the house. That's where people snoozed to get relief from the heat.

⓬ Some vineyards came with a watchtower to keep thieves away. The Book of Proverbs compares God to a fortified tower that protects the people.

⓭ Sheep provided wool that women wove into cloth on a loom. Jesus told his followers not to worry about the kind of clothes they wore. He said: "Is not . . . the body more than clothing?"

⓮ Writing was highly prized, and scrolls were frequently stored in earthenware jars so they would last a long time. God had commanded this in the Book of Jeremiah.

⓯ People ate from a common dish on the table. At the Last Supper, when Jesus said, "The one who has dipped his hand into the bowl will betray me," he was saying that Judas had just taken a helping.

15 GLITTERING FACTS ABOUT

❶ **The pharaoh** summoned Joseph from his dungeons **to explain the pharaoh's dream.** Pleased with Joseph's words, he put a **gold chain** around Joseph's neck.

❷ **Offerings of jewelry** were a good way to make up for your sins.

❸ The often criticized **Queen Jezebel,** wife of evil King Ahab, **painted her eyes with makeup** and adorned her head before she was thrown to her death.

❹ In his **Sermon on the Mount,** Jesus compared the Gospel to pearls and advised people not to **throw their pearls to the pigs** because they will trample them.

❺ **Jacob** feared that the earrings of his household members might be seen as symbols of false idols. **So he hid the jewels under an oak tree.**

❻ Desert tribesmen wore **earrings and necklaces.** Sometimes they used them to pay for room and board on a journey.

❼ **Signet rings** worn on the right hand were used to seal letters. The pharaoh gave Joseph his signet ring to express his favor.

❽ For the sin of pride, God took from the daughters of Zion (Jerusalem) "the anklets, the headbands, and the crescents; the pendants, the bracelets, and **the scarfs; the headdresses, the armlets,** the sashes, the perfume boxes, and the amulets."

FASHION

Bejeweled Egyptian woman from Fayoum, first century C.E.

9 To prepare for the **beauty contest** in which King Ahasuerus would choose a bride, a girl had to have beauty treatments for one year, including **six months of bathing in oils and perfumes.**

10 **King Solomon** praised his true love's beauty and adornment in the Song of Solomon. He told her that **her cheeks are beautiful with ornaments and her neck with strings of jewels.**

11 **Abraham** sent his servant to give Rebekah **two gold bracelets and a gold nose ring** as an offer of marriage from Abraham's son Isaac.

12 **Wealthy women bought hand mirrors** made from polished bronze.

13 A woman **poured pricey perfume** called *nard* over Jesus' head while he was in a leper's house. Some scolded her for wasting perfume **worth a year's wages.**

14 For **morning prayers,** Jews were commanded to bind small black leather boxes to their foreheads and upper arms with leather thongs. **Inside were biblical texts on parchment.**

15 As a **reward for hard work,** the Bible advised people to put on good clothes with a splash of cologne. If you were too poor to buy perfume, **olive oil would do.**

1 After the Israelites crossed the Red Sea from Egypt, Moses' sister, Miriam, took her **tambourine** and led the women in song and dance.

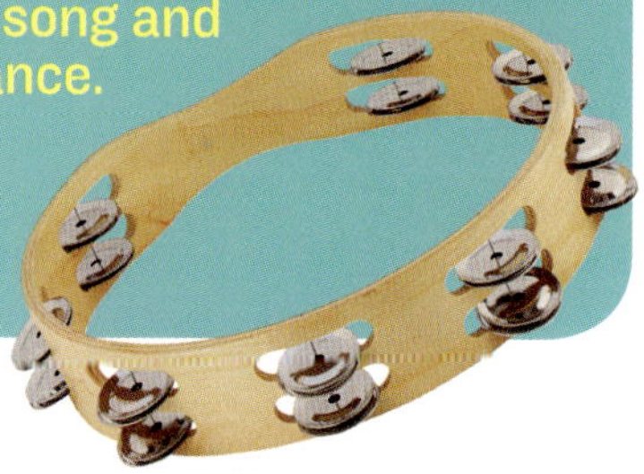

2 IN THE BOOK OF 1 SAMUEL, KING SAUL MET A GROUP OF PROPHETS WHO PROCLAIMED GOD'S WORD WHILE THEY PLAYED LYRES, TIMBRELS, PIPES, AND HARPS.

3 **THE PSALMS** were originally sung and accompanied by musical instruments. **KING DAVID** is thought to be the writer of many of them.

4 Many books in the Old Testament are written in short lines, or verses, like books of poetry. These include PSALMS, PROVERBS, and the SONG OF SOLOMON.

5 At the dedication ceremony for the Temple of Solomon, "the trumpeters and singers . . . (joined) in unison in praise and thanksgiving to the Lord."

25 HARMONIOUS FACTS ABOUT

6

"SING TO HIM A NEW SONG," declared the writer of Psalm 33 about praising God. "PLAY SKILLFULLY, ON THE STRINGS WITH LOUD SHOUTS."

7 In Luke's Gospel, the poem-like "Mary's Song of Praise," or "Magnificat," says, "My soul magnifies the Lord, / and my spirit rejoices in God my Savior."

8 One psalm instructed: "[M]ake a joyful noise to the Lord . . . with the lyre and the sound of melody, with trumpets and THE SOUND OF THE HORN."

9 SOME VERSES HAVE REPEATING STRUCTURE:
"The Lord is my . . . salvation;
whom shall I fear?
The Lord is the stronghold of my life;
of whom shall I be afraid?"

10 JOHN MILTON'S *PARADISE LOST* IS A **LONG POEM** BASED ON ADAM AND EVE, TELLING HIS VERSION OF HOW THEY HAD TO LEAVE THE GARDEN OF EDEN.

11 The Bible has inspired many poets. The poet **DANTE** wrote the ***Divine Comedy*** about his own spiritual journey from **HELL TO HEAVEN.**

12 THE MUSICAL PLAY ***GODSPELL***, ABOUT JESUS' LIFE, USED PSALMS AS ONE BASIS FOR ITS SONGS, INCLUDING THE PSALM OF PRAISE: **"BLESS THE LORD, OH MY SOUL."**

13 JEWISH CONGREGATIONS OFTEN **CHANT** PASSAGES FROM THE HEBREW BIBLE. THE SOUND HAS A SPECIAL TONE.

MUSIC AND POETRY

14

In 1 Chronicles, the Israelites brought out the ARK OF THE COVENANT to the sound of HORNS, TRUMPETS, CYMBALS, LYRES, AND HARPS.

15

ACCORDING TO THE OLD TESTAMENT, THE TALENTED PROPHET **Ezekiel** WAS LIKE "A SINGER OF LOVE SONGS, ONE WHO HAS A BEAUTIFUL VOICE AND PLAYS WELL ON AN INSTRUMENT."

16

A musician himself, King David told the Levites to **make a joyful sound with lyres, harps, and cymbals.**

17

KING NEBUCHADNEZZAR commanded three Jews to worship a gold idol when they heard "the horn, pipe, lyre, trigon, harp, drum, and entire musical ensemble."

18

UNLIKE MANY POEMS OR SONGS, BIBLE VERSES DON'T OFTEN RHYME— IN ENGLISH OR HEBREW.

19

When Paul and Silas were jailed by the Romans, THEY BURST INTO SONG AROUND MIDNIGHT praising God, and "prisoners were listening to them."

20

Author **Rudyard Kipling** wove nature into his poem "True Royalty," about biblical kings and queens: "... Solomon talked to a butterfly / As a man ... to a man."

21

"Sing psalms and hymns . . . to the Lord in your hearts," was the Apostle Paul's advice in a letter he sent to the Ephesians, people living in Ephesus.

22

WHEN KING SAUL WAS SAD, DAVID WOULD CHEER HIM UP BY PLAYING THE LYRE— A TYPE OF HARP.

23

In the Gospel of Matthew, following the Last Supper, Jesus' disciples sang a hymn together and then went out to the Mount of Olives.

24

THE BOOK OF JOB SAYS THAT WHEN GOD CREATED THE WORLD, THE MORNING STARS BEGAN TO SING TOGETHER AND ALL THE ANGELS SHOUTED FOR JOY.

25

The musical *Joseph and the Amazing Technicolor Dreamcoat* tells of Joseph, whose father gave him a coat; his jealous brothers sold him into slavery.

35 SICKENING FACTS

1. God sent TEN PLAGUES, each worse than the one before, until the pharaoh freed the Israelites from slavery.

2. In one plague, slimy, croaking frogs filled fields, houses, and beds. They died, and all of Egypt smelled like DEAD FROGS.

3. God sent FLIES into every crack and crevice in Egypt—except in Goshen, where the Israelites lived.

4. In another plague, LOCUSTS devoured every twig and blade of grass. Egypt lay in ruin, but Goshen stayed green.

5. In the last plague, God's angel killed every EGYPTIAN FIRSTBORN, even Pharaoh's. Israelite firstborns lived.

11. Deuteronomy warned that if the Israelites disobeyed God, he'd send "ULCERS, SCURVY, AND ITCH" that would not heal.

12. God also promised that disobedient people would "BE DRIVEN MAD by the sights you will see."

13. Sinners were warned that they might get DISEASES that would make them waste away.

14. Jesus cured a man of dropsy, a disease that made people PUFF UP LIKE A BALLOON from excess fluid.

15. God sent dysentery to King Jehoram for his evil actions: "HIS BOWELS CAME OUT . . . and he died in great agony."

21. God gave Miriam leprosy for talking against her brother Moses. She got "A FOUL FACE to match her foul mouth."

22. BROKEN ARMS were treated much as they are today, held by tight wrappings so they couldn't move.

23. Sometimes priests examined sick people. As long as they stayed sick, or "UNCLEAN," they were isolated from the community.

24. When King Asa's feet became diseased, he went to doctors, but didn't also ask God for help. His feet GOT WORSE.

25. Luke, an apostle of Jesus, was a DOCTOR. Actually, Jesus gave all his apostles the power to cure any illness.

A swarm of locusts darkens the sky.

ABOUT PLAGUES AND DISEASES

6. God ordered the Israelites to REGISTER at their sanctuary and pay a fee; if they didn't pay, they might suffer from a plague.

7. Moses' brother, Aaron, made a GOLD CALF for the Israelites to worship. God was angry and sent a plague.

8. God sent laws making the Israelites his special people. If they DISOBEYED, he would plague them "sevenfold."

9. In Revelation, John had visions of SEVEN ANGELS sending seven deadly plagues, including fire mixed with blood.

10. When the Israelites complained about wandering in the desert, God sent a plague that killed 14,700 people.

16. Epilepsy was sometimes called the "SACRED DISEASE." Some thought epileptics were possessed by demons.

17. Deuteronomy described FEVERS AND INFLAMMATION as sent from God for evil deeds.

18. Demons were often blamed for MENTAL HEALTH ISSUES. The Bible tells of a man who howled.

19. LEPROSY was feared because it deformed the skin and body; a person had to be isolated and became an outcast.

20. A sinner could expect to die from "consumption, fever, and inflammation." OBEDIENT people enjoyed good health.

26. In the Bible, prayer was often said to cure DISEASES, even snakebites.

27. In the New Testament, DEMONS were thought to cause some sickness. Priests "exorcised," or got rid of, them.

28. Many of the BLIND, MAIMED, AND DISEASED could only get food and clothes by begging at the roadsides.

29. The BALM OF GILEAD was an oil that was highly valued because it healed and soothed sick people.

30. The Prophet Isaiah ordered a poultice to be made from BOILED FIGS to cure King Hezekiah's serious illness.

31. The blind, lame, and paralyzed gathered at a pool near Jerusalem's Sheep Gate hoping AN ANGEL would cure them.

32. A TREATMENT for bleeding was to give God an offering of TWO TURTLEDOVES.

33. The Apostle Mark told how Jesus cured a woman who had BLED FOR 12 YEARS: She simply touched his cloak.

34. Egyptians EMBALMED, or drained and preserved, their dead. Jews wrapped the body in linen sprinkled with spices.

35. The Book of Proverbs says that "A CHEERFUL HEART is good medicine, but a downcast spirit dries up the bones."

15 REVEALING FACTS ABOUT

❶ **Jacob dreamed of a ladder to heaven** with angels climbing up and down it. God told Jacob that he would give him and his descendants a great nation in Egypt.

❷ Climbing Mount Sinai, Moses and the other elders of Israel had **a vision that God stood on sapphire-like stone.** God told Moses to go alone to the top to receive the Ten Commandments.

❸ **Zechariah** had eight night visions. In the first, he saw **red, brown, and white horses near myrtle trees.** An angel showed him they were sent to patrol the Earth.

❹ God told Moses that no one can see God's face and live, **so God covered Moses' eyes with a hand as He passed.** Moses saw only God's back.

❺ **Ezekiel had a vision** of God's chariot made up of wheels within wheels and four winged creatures with **four faces each: a cherub's, a human's, a lion's, and an eagle's.**

❻ **The angel Gabriel appeared to Mary** in Nazareth to tell her she had been chosen to be the mother of God's son.

❼ After Jesus' death, **an angel appeared to Mary Magdalene at Jesus' tomb** and rolled the rock from the entrance. The earth quaked and the angel said that Jesus had risen.

❽ **Saul was blinded by a vision of Jesus,** who appeared in a flash of light from heaven. When Jesus restored Saul's sight, scales fell from Saul's eyes. He became the Apostle Paul.

DREAMS AND VISIONS

"The Second Angel of the Apocalypse Creating a Storm," by Giusto di Giovanni de' Menabuoi, 1360–1370

❾ In a vision, Isaiah saw God on a throne, surrounded by angels. The hem of his robe filled the temple. One angel touched Isaiah's lips with a hot coal to blot out his sins.

❿ Daniel was frightened by his nightmare about four beasts. The most terrifying one had iron teeth, and a horn with humanlike eyes and a mouth that spoke.

⓫ In Revelation, John was terrified because he saw a vision of a Jesus he did not recognize, who appeared with eyes like flames, feet of bronze, and a sword coming out of his mouth.

⓬ In another vision, John saw God's throne room, in which there were four creatures. Each creature had six wings and was covered with eyeballs.

⓭ John had visions of death and destruction in sevens: He first saw seven angels with seven trumpets announcing ruin to the earth and stars; then seven angels sent seven deadly plagues.

⓮ John saw a battle in heaven between the angels and the devil as a dragon with seven heads and ten horns. The angels won and threw the devil to earth.

⓯ After his visions of death and destruction, John saw a new heaven and a new world as an angel showed him holy Jerusalem shining with "a radiance like a very rare jewel."

15 BUILDING FACTS

❶ **Joshua made a "tower" of 12 stones** to mark the place where the priests carried the Ark of the Covenant across the Jordan River in the Promised Land.

❷ To protect his capital, Jerusalem, against any enemies who might try to conquer it, King Uzziah built **three fortified towers** in the walls of the city.

❸ The builders of the **Tower of Babel** had lofty ambitions: They wanted it to **reach to the heavens.** It may have looked like a Mesopotamian ziggurat, a tower like a layer cake, with a temple on top.

❹ God was not impressed by the mighty walls of Babylon or the evil ways of its people. In the Book of Jeremiah, he said **the walls would be destroyed and their gates set on fire.**

❺ According to the Bible, 480 years after the Israelites left Egypt, **King Solomon began building his renowned temple to God** in Jerusalem. The site is thought to be Mount Moriah.

❻ The magnificent **temple of the goddess Artemis** was the pride of the city of Ephesus. Said the mayor: The image of the great Artemis "fell down to us from heaven."

❼ **Egypt's Pyramids of Giza, one of the Seven Wonders of the World,** were built from 2575 to 2150 B.C.E. They towered over the biblical Egypt of Abraham, Moses, and Joseph.

❽ The Israelites marched around the mighty wall of the city of Jericho. According to the Book of Joshua, **"The people shouted, and the trumpets were blown, and the wall fell down flat."**

OF THE BIBLICAL WORLD

The storerooms at King Herod's Masada fortress, Israel

❾ **The Herodium** was the winter palace and fortress of Herod the Great, built atop a cone-shaped hill 2,460 feet (750 m) above sea level; he may have been buried at the site.

❿ Called "the most magnificent building ever erected on earth," **King Nebuchadnezzar's Hanging Gardens of Babylon** had five courtyards and terraces that held one of every plant and tree in his empire.

⓫ **Masada was a Jewish fortress** built on a rock plateau 1,300 feet (396 m) above the Dead Sea and the Wilderness of Judea. Its remote location and steep cliffs made it a forbidding site.

⓬ **Caesarea Maritima was a great harbor and city** built by King Herod on the Mediterranean Sea. Peter baptized the Roman centurion Cornelius in the harbor.

⓭ King Cyrus of Babylon ordered **the rebuilding of Solomon's Temple,** destroyed by the previous king. This new "house of God" became the revered Temple of Jerusalem.

⓮ Joshua called **the fortress of Hazor** "the head of all [Canaanite] kingdoms." Archaeological remains show its magnificence.

⓯ In Genesis, Abraham bought **the Cave of Machpelah** to bury his wife Sarah. It is also known as the Cave of the Patriarchs, **the burial place of Abraham, Isaac, and Jacob.**

15 FACTS ABOUT NOAH AND

❶ According to the Book of Genesis, Noah was 600 years old when God told him to build the ark in order to escape the coming Flood.

❷ God gave Noah specific instructions for the ark: Make it out of some kind of wood (possibly cypress), divide it into rooms, and cover it inside and out with tar.

❸ The Hebrew word for "ark" is *teba*, which means "basket" or "chest."

❹ Noah's ark was a triple-decker, with three levels: lower, middle, and upper. The ark had only one door in and out.

❺ The ark was 300 cubits long, 50 cubits wide, and 30 cubits high. That's 450 feet (137 m) by 75 feet (23 m) by 45 feet (14 m)—the length of one and a half football fields.

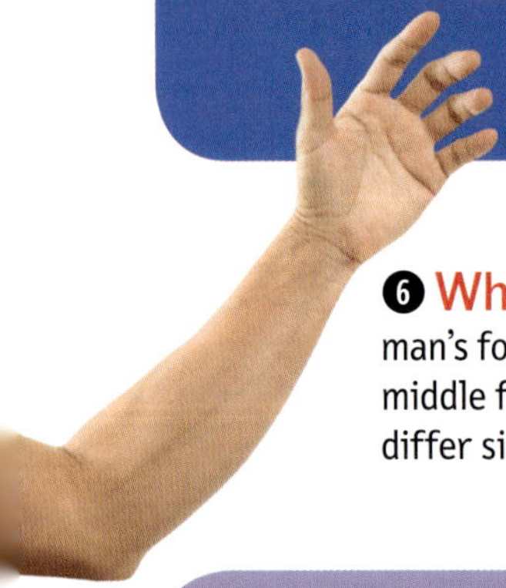

❻ What's a cubit? It's the length of a man's forearm, from his elbow to the tip of his middle finger: about 18 inches (46 cm). Cubits differ since all arms aren't the same length.

❼ The ark was a floating ship, not a sailing ship—it had no sails and no rudder.

❽ God told Noah to take two of every living thing on Earth with him into the ark—a male and female of every kind of bird, animal, and creeping thing.

HIS AWESOME ARK

Noah's ark mural, late 16th century C.E.

9 **How many people were on board** the ark with all those animals? **Just eight:** Noah, his wife, his three sons, and their wives.

10 Once the rain started, it didn't stop **for 40 days and 40 nights.**

11 A huge flood is sometimes called a **deluge,** which means an overwhelming amount of something. **In Noah's case, it was rain.**

12 When the rain stopped, **Noah sent out a dove,** but it returned because there was no dry place to land. **When the dove did not return, Noah knew it was safe to leave the ark.**

13 At God's command, **Noah brought all the animals out of the ark** onto the dry land so they could have babies and begin to fill the world again.

14 The search for Noah's ark is jokingly referred to as **"arkeology."** Get it?

15 Noah was old. According to Genesis, **Noah lived 350 years after the Flood.** If he were 600 when it started, that means he lived to the ripe old age of **950.**

15 MOUTHWATERING

❶ In the Book of Exodus, the Israelites ate a kind of bread called **manna.** It was white like coriander seed and **tasted like wafers made with honey.**

❷ During their wanderings in the desert, the Israelites missed the food they had in Egypt—**fish, cucumbers, melons, leeks, onions, and garlic.**

❸ God told his people that in the Promised Land they would find **"wheat and barley, vines and fig trees, pomegranates, olive trees and honey."**

❹ To celebrate bringing the Ark of the Covenant to Jerusalem, **King David gave out food** to everyone in Israel—**a loaf of bread, a portion of meat, and a cake of raisins.**

❺ One time, **Moses** entered the tent where God's laws were kept and saw that the walking stick of his brother, Aaron, **had sprouted and grown almonds.**

❻ **Nehemiah** described the foods that the people of Judah brought to sell in the capital, Jerusalem—**grain, wine, grapes, and figs.** The people of Tyre brought fish.

❼ "You shall not strip your vineyard bare, or gather the fallen grapes . . . ," God told his people in the Old Testament, but **"leave them for the poor and the alien."**

❽ When **Jacob** sent his sons to Egypt in the book of Genesis, he sent them with "some of the choice fruits of the land . . . : **honey, gum, resin, pistachio nuts, and almonds."**

FACTS ABOUT FOOD

Spice market in Istanbul, Turkey

❾ As they wandered in the desert, **the Israelites complained to God:** "Why have you brought us up out of Egypt ... to this wretched place [with no] grain, or figs, or vines, **or pomegranates."**

❿ In the Book of Leviticus, God told the Israelites **what kinds of food they could not eat,** including rabbits, pigs, and some kinds of seafood.

⓫ In the Gospel of John, **Jesus** described himself as the **"bread of life."** He said that anyone who believed in him would **never be hungry again.**

⓬ Jacob wanted to win the blessing of his father, Isaac, so he brought Isaac **a savory, or spicy, meal of two young goats** for a blessing ceremony.

⓭ When the crowd following him grew hungry, Jesus took **five loaves of bread and two fish** from a boy and turned them into **enough to feed 5,000 people.**

⓮ The Book of Psalms says that **God** causes "grass to grow for the cattle, and plants for people to use, **to bring forth food from the earth."**

⓯ **The prodigal son** lived a wasteful life and then came home to ask forgiveness. His father was so happy to see him that **he cooked a "fatted calf" to celebrate.**

35 FACTS ABOUT

1. People often **BARTERED,** or traded things they had, for things they needed, such as a goat for a sack of barley.

2. Early bartering usually took place at the **TOWN GATE,** where farmers and herders would trade with townspeople.

3. Before there was money as we know it today, people used **METAL PIECES OF SPECIFIC WEIGHTS** to buy things.

4. One weight was the **SHEKEL,** about the weight of two U.S. quarters. The verb *shaqal* means "to pay" and "to weigh."

5. The Bible mentions **SIX OTHER WEIGHTS** used for payment: talent, mina, beka, gerah, pim, and kesitah.

11. The military defenses and **CASTLES IN JERUSALEM** and other Muslim strongholds impressed Crusaders from Europe.

12. The most used coin in Jesus' day was the **SILVER *DENARIUS,*** about the size of a U.S. dime and worth a day's wage.

13. In the Bible, Jesus asked whose image and inscription was on the *denarius.* It was of the emperor, **CAESAR.**

14. Solomon imported **CHARIOTS** from Egypt for 600 shekels each and horses for 150 each from Kue, likely in Turkey.

15. **RAMS,** important for food and offerings, were an affordable purchase: They cost about two shekels each.

21. Abraham paid 400 shekels of silver for a tomb for his wife, Sarah—among the most **EXPENSIVE** buys in the Bible.

22. For 20 pieces of silver **JOSEPH'S BROTHERS SOLD HIM** to a caravan of traders going from Gilead to Egypt.

23. Around 640 B.C.E. the **FIRST COINS** were made in Lydia. Many were **ELECTRUM,** a natural mix of gold and silver.

24. The Jews made coins during their First Revolt against the Romans saying "Year 1 of the **REDEMPTION OF ISRAEL.**"

25. The chief priests paid Judas 30 silver coins to betray Jesus—**ABOUT FOUR MONTHS' WAGES.**

6

It would take a worker about 4 DAYS to earn one shekel, 3 months for a mina, and 15 years for a talent.

7

One million talents of silver and 100,000 talents of gold—$220 BILLION—was the cost for Solomon's Temple.

8

Solomon's YEARLY INCOME from taxes, gifts, and other sources would equal more than a billion dollars today.

9

Archaeologists found a bronze, TURTLE-SHAPED WEIGHT with the inscription "one-quarter shekel."

10

The CODE OF HAMMURABI, dating back to 1772 B.C.E., SET WAGES for all jobs and outlined banking regulations.

16

The variety of money coming into towns from trading with different city-states led to a new job: MONEY CHANGER.

17

Money changers used BENCHES drawn with lines and squares for calculating. "Bank" comes from *banco*, or bench.

18

The Bible forbid charging INTEREST on loans to the poor. Moses said this rule did not apply to foreigners.

19

Money changers often worked in temples. Jesus didn't like mixing business with worship and once DROVE THEM OUT.

20

Five lords of Philistine offered Delilah 1,100 SILVER PIECES to find out why Samson was strong, then betray him.

26

Many Bible passages warn people about money, such as "The love of money is THE ROOT OF ALL EVIL."

27

Phoenicians, from the Greek *phoinios*, or purple, were seagoing traders who TRADED PURPLE DYE to color cloth.

28

In the 700s B.C.E., round jugs transported wine and olive oil. They held HALF A HEKAT—two and a half quarts.

29

David was crowned king with a crown weighing "a talent of gold." That's 75 POUNDS (34 KG)!

30

BANKING began in Mesopotamia between 3000 and 2000 B.C.E., when bankers loaned grain to traders and farmers.

31

Jesus talked about leather purses wearing out. This could have happened, since bronze coins had SHARP EDGES.

32

The ancient KING'S HIGHWAY was used 2,000 years before Christ and still is used today in modern Jordan.

33

To warn of thieves on TRADE ROUTES, the Romans built forts and inns within SMOKE-SIGNALING distance of each other.

34

In 2012, a coin collector paid $1.1 million for a shekel made in 66 C.E. The metal was worth 26 CENTS.

35

When Jesus told Peter to fish, his first catch had four drachma in its mouth—the exact TEMPLE TAX they owed.

TRADE AND MONEY THAT YOU CAN BANK ON

15 REFRESHING FACTS ABOUT

1 Speaking through the Prophet Isaiah, God promised, "I will make the wilderness a pool of water, and the dry land springs of water."

2 The Prophet Daniel had a vision on the Tigris riverbank predicting the coming of God's son. The Tigris and Euphrates were the two major rivers of Mesopotamia.

3 The Sea of Galilee, where Jesus first met the Apostle Peter and his brother, Andrew, in the New Testament, is actually a freshwater lake. Today it is called Lake Kinneret.

4 At God's command, Moses lifted his staff, or walking stick, and struck it down on the waters of the Nile. As the pharaoh and his men watched, the water turned to blood.

5 In the Book of Genesis, God outlined for Abraham the borders of the Promised Land. The northern limit was marked by the "great river," the Euphrates.

6 Angry with King Ahab, God sent the Prophet Elijah to tell him that it would not rain for many years. Then God sent Elijah to hide near a brook and drink from it until it ran dry.

7 To hide her baby from the Egyptians, Moses' mother put him in a woven basket and set it among the papyrus reeds on the bank of the Nile River.

Jesus walks on the Sea of Galilee.

BODIES OF WATER

❽ Lot moved to the Jordan Valley, where it was "well-watered everywhere like the Garden of the Lord."

❾ After the servant Hagar ran away, an angel found her near a spring of water and told her two things: to go home and to name her son Ishmael.

❿ The first river in the Bible is in the Garden of Eden: "A river flows out of Eden to water the garden, and from there it divides and becomes four branches."

⓫ The Gospel of Mark opens with John the Baptist preaching in the wilderness. People from Jerusalem traveled out to hear him, and he baptized them in the Jordan River.

⓬ During their wanderings in the desert, the Israelites came to a place named Elim, where "there were twelve springs and seventy palm trees, and they camped . . . near the water."

⓭ At the end of the New Testament, in the Book of Revelation, the devil is thrown into a lake of fire and sulfur.

⓮ When two men possessed by demons confronted Jesus, he ordered the demons to enter a herd of pigs. The pigs rushed into the sea and drowned.

⓯ The pharaoh dreamed that seven healthy cows and seven thin cows came out of the Nile River. Joseph said it meant that Egypt would have seven years of plenty and seven of famine.

15 BLISTERING FACTS

❶ In the Hebrew Bible, "wilderness" sometimes means "desert." It was challenging to survive in these barren wastelands that were often without water or plants.

❷ Moses and the Israelites spent 40 years lost in the Sinai desert after they escaped Egypt.

❸ Moses and the Israelites went three days without water in the Shur desert.

❹ When Moses' sister, Miriam, died, she was buried in the Desert of Zin.

❺ In the Desert of Zin, Moses struck a rock twice with his staff, making water flow for the thirsty people and livestock.

❻ Abraham sent his slave Hagar and the son she bore him, Ishmael, into the desert because Abraham's wife did not want Ishmael to receive her own son's inheritance.

❼ Ishmael grew up in the Desert of Paran and became an accomplished archer, skilled with a bow and arrow.

Camel caravan in the desert

ABOUT THE DESERT

8 King Saul, with 3,000 men, chased David in the **Desert of En-gedi** and searched for him in craggy, near-impassable areas, like **Rocks of the Wild Goats.**

9 **An oasis** is an area in the desert where plants grow, thanks to an underground spring or other water source. **Oases were welcome sights for travelers and traders.**

10 **Many battles were fought to control oases,** The best known was the **Battle of Kadesh,** between two powers of the 13th century B.C.E.: the Egyptians and the Hittites.

11 **John the Baptist traveled through the desert** preaching that baptism was a way to repent for sins.

12 One proverb claimed that it is **better to live in a desert than with a quarrelsome woman.**

13 **A wadi** can be a riverbed in the desert that fills with water only during heavy rains. **When dry, wadis became roads for traders and travelers.**

14 Jesus fasted for **40 days and 40 nights in the desert,** then was tempted by the devil. When Jesus refused him, the devil left and angels came.

15 About 45 days after they left Egypt, the Israelites reached a place called **the Desert of Sin,** on the way to Mount Sinai.

15 INSPIRATIONAL FACTS

❶ Sometimes called the poor man's Bible, colorful **stained-glass windows** featuring stories from the Bible were created in Europe during the Middle Ages to reach people who **couldn't read.**

❷ Early Christians made **wall paintings based on Bible stories in catacomb churches.** Catacombs were underground tunnels dug as burial places. Christians prayed there, hidden from disapproving officials.

❸ Colorful **wall murals painted along the streets of Los Angeles,** California, U.S.A., show the Last Supper and Judas betraying Jesus with a kiss.

❹ Archaeologists uncovered a **mosaic in Israel** showing the Bible hero Samson. He is tying torches to the tails of foxes so **they'll burn the fields of his enemy as they run through them.**

❺ The French artist **Paul Gauguin** painted "The Yellow Christ" in 1889, showing the Crucifixion taking place not in the Holy Land, but in his country, in the 19th century.

❻ From 1508 to 1512, the Italian artist Michelangelo painted the ceiling of the **Sistine Chapel in Rome** with scenes from Genesis. He painted lying flat on his back, on scaffolding high above the ground.

❼ Many churches in Eastern Europe feature **icons—images on wood, paintings, embroidery, or mosaics—**that show biblical figures like Jesus, Mary, or the angels.

Detail from "The Creation of Adam" on the Sistine Chapel ceiling, by Michelangelo, 1511–1512

ABOUT BIBLICAL ART

8 Inspired by the Bible, **Michelangelo sculpted the "Pietà."** It shows Mary cradling Jesus' body after the Crucifixion, something not mentioned in the Bible.

9 When Dutch artist **Vincent van Gogh** painted "The Good Samaritan" in 1890, he was in a hospital. The painting was inspired by the Apostle Luke's parable about **helping a stranger in need.**

10 The modern artist **Marc Chagall** created stained-glass windows showing the 12 tribes of Israel that now illuminate the chapel in the **Hadassah Hospital** in Jerusalem.

11 Jesus' Last Supper is **carved into many altars, including a wooden altar** in a church in Rothenburg, Germany.

12 Artists for the animated film ***The Prince of Egypt*** sketched thousands of images of Moses and Ramses, portrayed as his adoptive brother, to make them move **on-screen.**

13 The **Italian artist Caravaggio** was a troublemaker. His patron refused to pay him for a version of St. Matthew and the angel because it was disrespectful: **He had painted Matthew with dirty feet.**

14 Guatemalan folk artists create ***santos*—colorful pottery statues** of Jesus, Mary, and saints from the Bible.

15 Italian artist **Leonardo da Vinci** painted the mural "The Last Supper" in the 1490s in a convent in Italy. It portrays the moment when the Apostles learned that **one of them would betray Jesus.**

1

Priests laid their hands on a goat's head to confess the people's sins. The goat was then taken to the wilderness. The word **"scapegoat"** comes from this.

2

TO SEARCH "THE FOUR CORNERS OF THE EARTH" MEANS TO LOOK EVERYWHERE. ISAIAH PREDICTED THAT AT THE END OF TIME, GOD'S PEOPLE WILL GATHER FROM THESE CORNERS.

3

If something happens fast, it's **"IN THE TWINKLING OF AN EYE."** The phrase in the Bible tells how quickly humans will become immortal at the end of time.

4

A **"DOUBTING THOMAS"** has to see something to believe it. The Apostle Thomas wouldn't believe Jesus had risen from the dead until he touched Jesus' wounds.

5

If you see **"THE WRITING ON THE WALL,"** there's trouble ahead. Wicked King Belshazzar saw God's hand writing on the palace wall, predicting his **RUIN.**

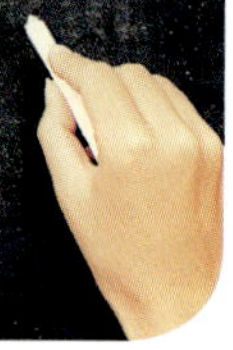

25 FACTS ABOUT

6

God soothed his people by saying that all nations combined were only **"a drop in the bucket"** compared to God's universe. This still means a tiny amount.

7

Job LISTED ALL THE BAD THINGS THAT HAD HAPPENED TO HIM, AND CRIED THAT HE'D ESCAPED **"by the skin of his teeth"—** MEANING HE ALMOST HADN'T MADE IT.

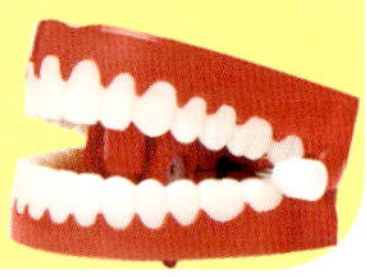

8

"Out of the mouth of babes" means that children speak the truth. It comes from the Book of Psalms, which suggests that EVEN INFANTS SING GOD'S PRAISE.

9

Someone loved above all others would be considered **"THE APPLE OF MY EYE."** God used this term for the Israelites.

10

IN EARLY BIBLE LAW, **"AN EYE FOR AN EYE"** MEANT THAT YOU COULD NOT HURT A PERSON MORE THAN HE HURT YOU. JESUS LATER SAID **"turn the other cheek,"** OR DON'T FIGHT BACK.

11

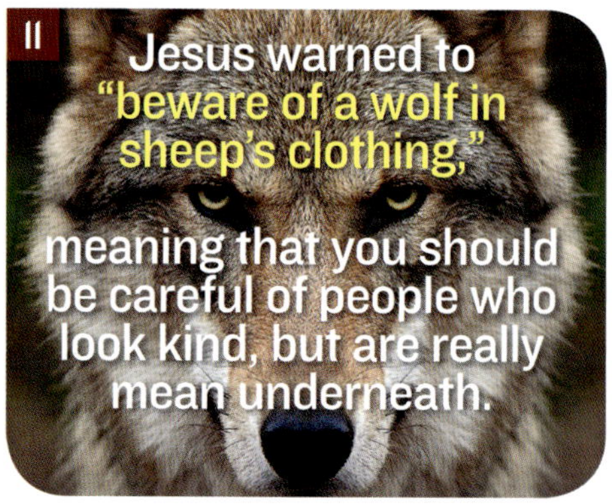

Jesus warned to **"beware of a wolf in sheep's clothing,"** meaning that you should be careful of people who look kind, but are really mean underneath.

12

A **"FLY IN THE OINTMENT"** is a tiny problem that could ruin a bigger plan. Ointments in biblical times were lotions or oils that made a ceremony sacred.

BIBLE EXPRESSIONS

13

The age-old question, "Can people change who they really are?" is answered by this question in the BOOK OF JEREMIAH: "Can a leopard change its spots?"

14

"Old as the hills" may come from the wise man Eliphaz's question to Job: "Are you the firstborn of the human race . . . brought forth before the hills?"

15

If someone is "AT WIT'S END" with you, watch out. They've run out of all patience and they have no idea what to do.

16

THE TERM "bite the dust" COMES FROM A PRAYER ASKING GOD TO ENSURE THAT SOLOMON'S ENEMIES WILL "LICK THE DUST," OR FALL DEAD OR WOUNDED IN BATTLE.

17

"A bird in the hand is better than two in the bush" has roots in a Bible passage that means it is better to be sure of a little than to hope for a lot.

18

WHEN SOMETHING IS OFF-LIMITS, WE SAY IT'S "FORBIDDEN FRUIT," LIKE THE FRUIT IN THE GARDEN OF EDEN.

19

Apples aren't in the Bible, but now symbolize the forbidden fruit. The bulge in a male's throat is called an "Adam's apple," as if an apple is stuck in it.

20

Who wouldn't want to "eat, drink, and be merry"? A verse in Ecclesiastes said that having fun, along with working hard, is part of each day.

21

"A person after my own heart" is someone who is a lot like you. God declared King David a man after his own heart, who would carry out his wishes.

22

A person called to spread the Christian faith is said to "FIGHT THE GOOD FIGHT." You might use the expression when you want to do the right thing.

23

In the Bible, a person without sin was said to be "WHITE AS SNOW," or pure.

24

"Who am I to cast the first stone?" means people should not judge others. Jesus kept a mob from stoning a woman by saying only a non-sinner could throw the first stone.

25

THE GOOD SAMARITAN WAS A TRAVELER WHO HELPED A MAN HURT BY A ROBBER. TODAY, GOOD SAMARITAN LAWS PROTECT PEOPLE WHO HELP STRANGERS IN TROUBLE.

15 TONGUE-TWISTING FACTS

1 Ever heard someone exclaim **"Jumpin' Jehoshaphat"**—and wonder who Jehoshaphat was? He was **an Old Testament king of Judah.**

2 You've heard of the Prophet **Isaiah. His name is easy to say three times fast.** Now try the names of these less well known prophets: **Zephaniah, Obadiah, and Habakkuk.**

3 **Maher-shalal-hash-baz**—Isaiah's son—had the longest name in the Bible. It means **"rapid plunder,"** or "destroy and steal it fast!" The name foretold war between Israel and Assyria.

4 **Moses** may have had trouble saying even the simplest words. He once told God, **"I am slow of speech and tongue."**

5 **King Nebuchadnezzar** was named after a Babylonian god. His name means **"Nebo, protect the crown."**

6 When **Joseph** arrived in Egypt, Pharaoh gave him an Egyptian name—**Zaphenath-Paneah.** Some think it means "revealer of secrets," but experts aren't sure.

7 **Zechariah became tongue-tied** because he didn't believe an angel who told him his wife, Elizabeth, would have a child. When she gave birth to **John the Baptist,** Zechariah could talk again.

8 At the Tower of Babel, **God changed the single language of the people into many languages** so they couldn't understand each other.

ABOUT BIBLICAL WORDS

Detail from "Belshazzar's Feast," by Rembrandt van Rijn, 1637

9 ***MENE, MENE, TEKEL, PARSIN*** were the words God wrote on the palace wall of Babylon's King Belshazzar. They told the king that **God was going to end his reign.**

10 The Israelites **Sheshbazzar,** then Zerubbabel, grandson of Jehoiachin, **helped rebuild the Temple of Jerusalem** after it was destroyed by Nebuchadnezzar, King of Babylon. You won't hear those names every day.

11 King Saul's grandson **Mephibosheth** was disabled. **When he was a baby, his nurse had dropped him** while running to safety during a battle.

12 In the New Testament, **Jesus healed a man who was a deaf-mute**—he couldn't hear or speak. **Jesus put his fingers into the man's ears and touched his tongue.**

13 The Prophet **Daniel** was also brought to serve Babylon's king. **Daniel's new name was Belteshazzar.** That's a long one!

14 When the Israelites **Hananiah, Mishael, and Azariah** became servants to Babylon's king, he renamed them something harder to say: **Shadrach, Meshach, and Abednego.**

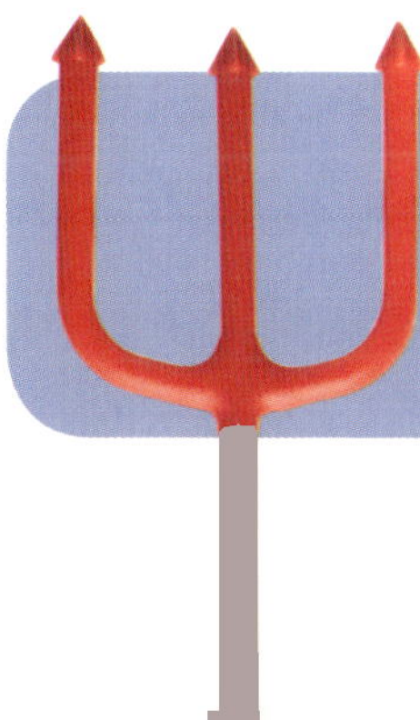

15 The name **Beelzebul,** from Baal-zebub, an ancient Philistine god, meant "lord of the flies." It is also used for the prince of demons, sometimes simply called **the devil.**

1

The **Book of Numbers** is the fourth book of the Old Testament. In it, God tells Moses to take the first official **census,** or count, of the Israelites.

2

The census also counted the **number of males,** 20 years and older, able to go to war. The tribe of Judah had the most: **74,600 young men.**

3

When tracing Jesus' family history, the Book of Matthew says there were **42 generations** from Abraham to Jesus.

4

A measure of **one cubit** equaled the length of a man's forearm, about **18 inches** (46 cm).

5

A **handbreadth** was the width of three fingers, or **three inches (7.5 cm).**

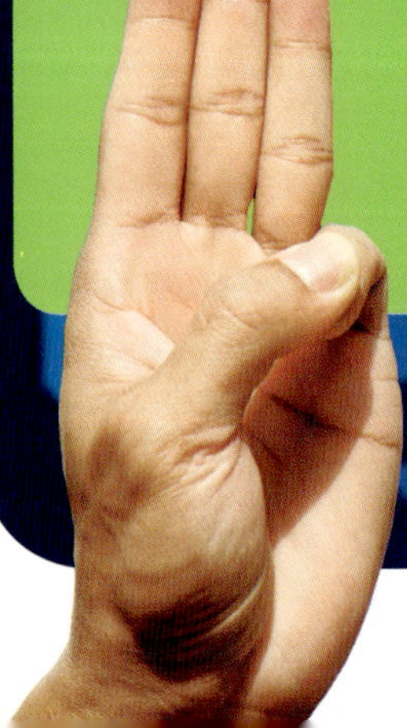

6

The **Temple of Jerusalem** was 60 cubits long, 20 cubits wide, and 30 cubits high—that's 90 feet by 30 feet by 45 feet (27.5 m by 9 m by 14 m).

7

King Solomon had at least **700 wives and 300 concubines;** many of them got him into trouble with God because they worshipped foreign gods.

8

The full Bible has been translated into more than **1,000 languages.**

9

The Bible claims that King Solomon wrote **1,005 songs and 3,000 proverbs,** or pieces of advice, such as "beauty is useless in a woman who has no common sense."

10

Food and other items were **measured in containers** holding these amounts: a cor, about six bushels; a bath, about six gallons; and a log, about two cups.

11

Moses' older brother, **Aaron,** was Moses' spokesman for almost **40 years.**

12

More than **6 billion Bibles** have been printed. Each year, 100 million Bibles are sold, meaning an average of **250,000 Bibles are sold each day.**

13

How many Israelites did Moses lead from Egypt? Scholars estimate **2.5 to 3 million people.**

14

The Tabernacle tent that held the Ark of the Covenant was made out of **ten fine-linen curtains,** all 28 cubits long and 4 cubits wide.

15

According to Genesis, **Noah's ark** was 50 cubits wide, 30 cubits high, and 300 cubits—about one and a half football fields—long.

16

Some judges had big families: Ibzan had **30 sons and 30 daughters.** He swapped the daughters for 30 wives for his sons.

17

The Book of Psalms is the longest book by far in the Bible, with **150 chapters.** Each chapter is a psalm, or sacred song.

18

The Bible's **first English translation** was in 1382 C.E. by John Wycliffe.

19

The Bible was originally written in **three languages—**Hebrew, Aramaic, and Koine Greek, which was used by most people living east of Egypt.

20

The Bible was the **first book printed** on Johannes Gutenberg's printing press in 1454 C.E.

21

The oldest man in the Bible is Noah's grandfather Methuselah: **He was 969!**

22

There are more than **12 prophetic books** in the Old Testament. Many warn what happens if people ignore God, but they promise God's forgiveness, too.

23

There are **13 men** in the Old Testament named Obadiah, "servant of God" in Hebrew.

24

Solomon's Temple took **seven years to build** by 30,000 Israelites and 150,000 others, including 30,000 log cutters, 80,000 stonecutters, and 70,000 stone carriers.

25

In Revelation, Jesus opens four seals on a scroll held by God, and four horsemen appear on horses. Some call them the **Four Horsemen of the Apocalypse.**

26

The Geneva Bible was the first English Bible to be divided by chapter and verse. It was among the Bibles that came to America on the *Mayflower* in 1620.

27

In the Bible, **many things come in twos:** Animals enter the ark in pairs; two angels guard the Ark of the Covenant; and the disciples have a buddy system.

28

Ecclesiastes says to value friends because **"two are better than one.** If either falls down one can help the other up."

29

Gematria is a system that assigns numbers to Greek and Hebrew words. Some numbers were believed to be lucky, such as **888,** the Greek gematria for Jesus.

30

The Hebrew gematria number for the beast, or devil, was determined to be **666.**

50 Fabulous Facts About NUMBERS and FIGURES

31
The New Testament says Jesus rose from the dead **three days** after his Crucifixion.

32
When soldiers arrested Jesus, the disciple Peter denied knowing him **three times.**

33
The number four often related to earth and nature. Daniel had a vision that four winds stirred up the sea and released four monsters.

34
Three main virtues, or human qualities, highlighted by Paul in his letter to the Corinthians are **faith, hope, and love.**

35
In a vision, John saw **200 million soldiers** with lionlike heads, on horseback, wearing fire-colored breastplates, and breathing fire and smoke.

36
The river that watered the Garden of Eden divided into **four branches** outside the garden: the Pishon, the Gihon, the Tigris, and the Euphrates.

37
After performing a miracle with five loaves and two fish, Jesus had enough food to feed **5,000 people.**

38
Forlorn and full of sorrow and shame, Judas threw out the **30 pieces of silver** he was paid for betraying Jesus into the temple.

39
After his shipmates threw Jonah overboard to calm the raging sea, Jonah spent **three days and three nights** in the belly of a great fish.

40
Shevah is the **Hebrew word for the number seven.** From it comes "Sabbath." The number also represents completion, such as the end of the week.

41
God rested on the **seventh day** because all of the work was done.

42
A large gold lamp stood in front of the Temple of Jerusalem. It had a stem and **six branches:** three off to one side, and three off to the other.

43
Pharaoh dreamed of **seven fat cows, and seven scrawny cows.** Joseph said it meant Egypt would have seven years of plenty, then seven years of famine.

44
Jesus told Peter that if someone hurts you, you must forgive not 7 times, but **77 times,** meaning that you should never stop forgiving.

45
According to the Bible, God's promises are so pure that they are like **silver refined in a furnace seven times**—a process to remove impurities.

46
Paul talked about the **nine desires of the spirit:** love, joy, peace, patience, kindness, generosity, faithfulness, gentleness, and self-control.

47
To cure Mary Magdalene of all evil, **Jesus cast out seven demons** from her.

48
The Prophet Ahijah **tore his cloak into 12 pieces,** signifying the 12 tribes of Israel. Ten pieces went to Solomon's servant Jeroboam, who would be king of **10 tribes.**

49
An angel said the new Jerusalem would have a wall with **12 gates** guarded by **12 angels** and inscribed with the names of Israel's **12 tribes.**

50
Jesus' mother, Mary, may be the woman in Revelation with a **crown of 12 stars.**

25 MOVING FACTS ABOUT

1 Abraham journeyed with his clan from the **CITY OF UR** of the Chaldees to Haran and onward to the land of Canaan, a distance of about **1,000 miles (1,600 km).**

2 THE **THREE WISE MEN,** OR MAGI, WERE KINGS WHO JOURNEYED MORE THAN **1,000 MILES (1,600 KM)** FROM THEIR LANDS EAST OF JERUSALEM: ARABIA, PERSIA, AND INDIA.

3 **JOSEPH AND MARY** traveled about **100 miles (160 km)** from their hometown, Nazareth, to Bethlehem, to be counted in a census. In Bethlehem, Mary gave birth to Jesus.

4 The enemy took Abraham's nephew, Lot, from Sodom, **so Abraham led 318 soldiers to rescue him, marching to the city of Dan** and then north of Damascus.

5 TO OBEY GOD'S COMMAND TO SACRIFICE HIS SON ISAAC, ABRAHAM TOOK ISAAC ON A **50-MILE (80-KM), THREE-DAY TRIP BY DONKEY** FROM BEERSHEBA TO THE LAND OF MORIAH.

6 MARY AND JOSEPH **FLED** WITH BABY JESUS **TO EGYPT.** KING HEROD HAD HEARD OF A NEW KING FROM THE MAGI AND **ordered all infant males killed to protect his throne.**

7 When an angel told her that an older relative, Elizabeth, was pregnant, too, Mary traveled nearly **70 MILES (113 KM)** to share the joys of upcoming motherhood.

8 **Nehemiah** WAS A CUPBEARER FOR THE KING OF PERSIA. WHEN HE HEARD THAT HIS HOME CITY, **JERUSALEM,** HAD BURNED DOWN, HE TRAVELED **900 MILES (1,450 KM) TO REBUILD ITS GATES.**

9 **Saul** was searching the hills near Mount Ephraim for his father's donkeys when the Prophet Samuel walked up and made him the first KING OF THE ISRAELITES.

10 The Prophet **Deborah went from her home** near Bethel to help lead the Israelites against King Jabin of Hazor in the Jezreel Valley. **She predicted their win.**

11 **The Israelites carried the Ark of the Covenant hundreds of miles** from Egypt to Gilgal to Shiloh to Gibeon, and at last to Solomon's Temple in Jerusalem.

12 YOUNG DAVID JOURNEYED ABOUT 15 MILES (24 KM) FROM BETHLEHEM TO THE **VALLEY OF ELAH, OR "OAK,"** TO FIGHT THE FEARSOME GIANT GOLIATH.

13 BECAUSE OF FAMINE, NAOMI AND HER FAMILY LEFT BETHLEHEM FOR MOAB, A WALK THAT TOOK ABOUT SEVEN DAYS ON FOOT.

14

MANY TRIPS WERE BY MERCHANTS ON SHIPS. A passage in Ezekiel lists several towns and the goods they traded with merchants from the COASTAL TOWN OF TYRE.

15

JOURNEYS DURING BIBLICAL TIMES WERE FILLED WITH DANGERS— WILD ANIMALS, BANDITS, STORMS, AND FLOODS.

16

WAR was perhaps the most common reason for a journey. SOLDIERS TRAVELED THROUGHOUT CANAAN TO GAIN CONTROL AND MAINTAIN ORDER.

17

Messengers TRAVELED THOUSANDS OF MILES THROUGH THE ANCIENT WORLD, CARRYING MESSAGES BY FOOT, OR ON HORSEBACK.

18

Paul's travels to spread the word of Jesus were tough. He was imprisoned, beaten, stoned, SHIPWRECKED, COLD, starved, parched, and EXHAUSTED.

JOURNEYS

19

MANY JEWS TRAVELED TO JERUSALEM EACH YEAR TO CELEBRATE THE FESTIVAL OF PASSOVER. FOR JESUS AND HIS FAMILY, THE TRIP FROM NAZARETH WAS ABOUT 100 MILES (160 KM).

20

During biblical times, FESTIVALS in Shechem, Shiloh, Bethel, Dan, and Jerusalem drew people from all over ancient Israel. Some traveled many miles.

21

Merchants' camel caravans with gum, resin, and balm went from Canaan to Egypt, more than 300 miles (480 km). They stayed in groups to guard against bandits and beasts.

22

The Apostle Paul took four missionary trips to preach Jesus' Gospel. On the first trip, he founded the first non-Jewish church in ANTIOCH OF PISIDIA.

23

ON PAUL'S SECOND TRIP, HE AND HIS COMPANION WERE THROWN IN JAIL IN PHILIPPI. THEY COULD HAVE ESCAPED, BUT DIDN'T WANT TO GET THE JAILER IN TROUBLE.

24

Jesus and his disciples traveled mostly by foot. Jesus once walked some 40 MILES (64 KM) from Nazareth to Capernaum, a town on the north shore of the Sea of Galilee.

DETOUR

25

Even though Moses promised they wouldn't leave the KING'S HIGHWAY, the Israelites were DENIED PASSAGE through the kingdom of Edom on the way to Canaan.

25 VILLAINOUS FACTS AND

1

IN THE BOOK OF ACTS, PAUL'S ENEMIES WERE SO DESPERATE TO KILL HIM THAT THEY SWORE AN OATH NOT TO EAT OR DRINK UNTIL HE WAS DEAD.

2

The snake told Eve to eat the fruit in the Garden of Eden. "You will not die," he said. "God knows that if you eat the fruit … you will be like God …"

3

WHEN HER FATHER, LABAN, WAS OUT SHEARING SHEEP, **Rachel stole the idols he worshipped.** THEN SHE AND HER HUSBAND, JACOB, PACKED UP AND LEFT.

4

Saul gave David his oldest daughter to marry if David would "fight the Lord's battles" against the Philistines. Secretly, HE HOPED DAVID WOULD DIE.

5

When a hungry Esau asked Jacob for A BOWL OF STEW, Jacob gave it to him only when Esau promised he could inherit ALL THEIR FATHER'S PROPERTY.

6

HAMAN, a powerful official for the king of Persia, ORDERED ALL THE JEWS IN PERSIA KILLED because the queen's cousin, Mordecai, would not bow to him.

7

CAIN WAS ANGRY WHEN GOD ACCEPTED THE OFFERING OF HIS BROTHER ABEL, BUT NOT HIS. SO CAIN ASKED ABEL TO GO OUT TO A FIELD WITH HIM, THEN KILLED HIM.

8

PONTIUS PILATE said of Jesus, "I am innocent of this man's blood." HE WASHED HIS HANDS, a sign that the crowd could do with Jesus what they wanted.

9

Before Saul became the Apostle Paul, he allowed Jesus' disciple **Stephen to be stoned to death,** and searched houses to imprison other disciples.

10

WHEN SAUL DIED, HIS SON ISHBAAL WAS CROWNED KING OF ISRAEL. ARMY OFFICERS FOUND HIM RESTING, STABBED HIM, CUT OFF HIS HEAD, AND CARRIED IT AWAY.

11

THE SATAN (devil) said that if Job lost his wealth and his children he would reject God. God took them all and more, but **Job kept his faith.**

12

King David's son **ABSALOM** WAS POWER HUNGRY. Each day at the gates of Jerusalem, he worked to convince people he'd be a better judge than David.

13 AFTER HE REFUSED TO LET THE ISRAELITES LEAVE EGYPT, THE PHARAOH **FORCED THEM TO MAKE BRICKS** AND GATHER THE BRICK-MAKING MATERIALS, TOO.

14 When Jesus was close to death on the Cross, he asked for **water.** Roman soldiers soaked **a sponge with sour wine** and gave it to him.

15 Abimelech, a son of the judge and leader Gideon, had **70 BROTHERS.** He tried to kill them all so he could be king. One lived, and later was king.

16 The sick beggar Lazarus sat at the gate of a rich man each day, asking for food as the dogs licked his sores. **The man ignored him.**

17 One woman was so determined to keep another woman's baby that when Solomon suggested they should cut the baby in half to share it, **she agreed!**

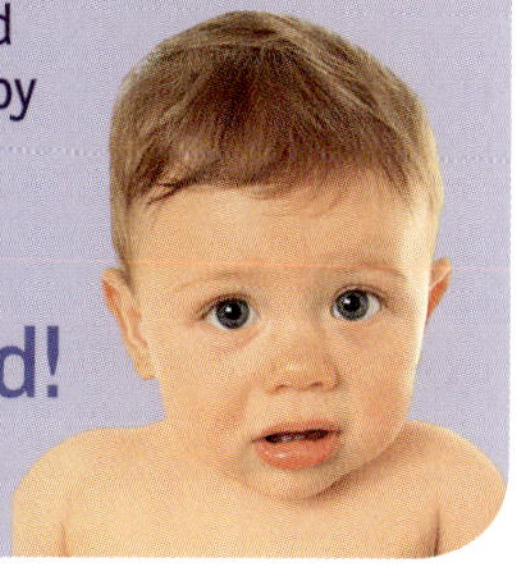

18 **QUEEN ATHALIAH** is the only woman monarch in the Bible. When her son died, she ORDERED HER GRANDSONS MURDERED SO SHE COULD TAKE THE THRONE.

DASTARDLY DEEDS

19

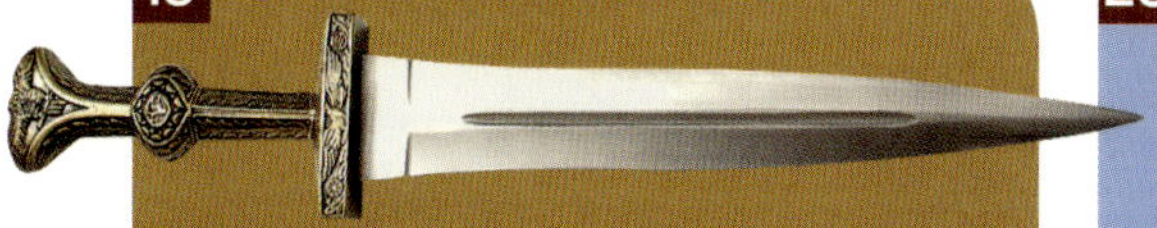

In the Book of 2 Samuel, a military officer named **JOAB BETRAYED A RIVAL,** Amasa, and stabbed him in the belly WITH A DAGGER.

20 JOSEPH'S JEALOUS BROTHERS FIRST WANTED TO KILL HIM, **BUT SOLD HIM TO TRADERS INSTEAD.** THEY LIED TO THEIR FATHER THAT HE WAS EATEN BY WILD ANIMALS.

21 After the time of Joseph, a new pharaoh in Egypt mistreated the Israelites, FORCING THEM "TO ABANDON THEIR INFANTS SO THAT THEY WOULD DIE."

22 **David** WAS IN LOVE WITH URIAH'S WIFE, SO HE SENT URIAH INTO BATTLE, KNOWING HE WOULD BE KILLED.

23 **ROMAN SOLDIERS** blindfolded Jesus so he couldn't **SEE, AND BEGAN TO HIT HIM.** Then they mocked him **BY TELLING HIM TO PROPHESY** who had hit him.

24 In Gethsemane, Judas identified Jesus to the Roman guards by giving him a kiss. The guards arrested Jesus and gave Judas **30 PIECES OF SILVER.**

25 GOD TOLD ABRAHAM THAT HE WOULD NOT DESTROY THE WICKED PEOPLE OF SODOM IF ABRAHAM COULD FIND EVEN **TEN GOOD PEOPLE** IN THE CITY. **HE COULD NOT.**

1

Deborah was the only woman judge mentioned in the Bible. She would sit under a palm tree and the Israelites would come to her for judgment.

2

Deborah was also a warrior who led 10,000 soldiers into battle.

3

Judith was a beautiful widow. She helped save her people by befriending the enemy general, then cutting off his head with his sword.

4

Judith stood up to Israelite officials who challenged God to protect them from the Assyrian enemy. She said, "Who are you to put God to the test?"

5

The angel Gabriel told Mary that she would bear God's son, the Messiah, or Savior of the Jews.

6

Jesus' mother, Mary, was important to him throughout his life. To Christians she is the most respected female figure in the Bible.

7

After Jesus healed the wealthy Joanna, she sold her property to help the poor and gave money to support Jesus and his apostles.

8

Astarte was a Canaanite goddess whom King Solomon worshipped along with God. This angered God, so he made sure the Israelites were defeated.

9

Jael killed the Canaanite army commander by driving a tent peg through his head as he slept. The Israelites celebrated his death by this brave woman.

10

To visit the king of Persia without being summoned could mean death. Esther risked her life to beg him to save the Jews of Persia. The feast Purim honors her.

11

The Queen of Sheba gave Solomon camels loaded with spices, gold, and precious stones. In return, she asked him to share his wisdom.

12

Hagar was the only person to name God. She called him El-Roi, "the God who sees."

13

Two midwives risked death by defying Pharaoh's order to kill Hebrew baby boys.

14

Pharaoh's daughter adopted Moses, even though she knew he was a Hebrew baby.

15

Ruth, David's great-grandmother, was kind, brave, and loyal. To help her widowed mother-in-law, she left her homeland and went to Bethlehem.

16

The 84-year-old widow Anna was a prophet who foretold stories about Jesus.

17

Queen Athaliah is the only Judean woman monarch in the Bible.

18

The wise woman of Tekoa disguised herself and told King David a story to convince him to spare the life of his son who had killed his other son.

19

Samson loved Delilah, but she betrayed him. She discovered that the source of his strength was his hair and had his head shaved in his sleep.

20

The Bible does not say that Eve told Adam to take a bite of the forbidden fruit, but he probably followed her example.

21

Priscilla traveled with the Apostle Paul to Syria as a missionary. There she taught the gifted speaker Apollos what she had learned from Paul.

22

The disciple Tabitha served the poor. She died and Peter raised her from the dead.

23

Mary Magdalene stayed with Jesus during his Crucifixion. John was the only other apostle brave enough to remain with her; the rest fled.

24

Mary Magdalene was the first person Jesus appeared to after his Resurrection. He called to her and she answered "Rabbouni," Aramaic for "teacher."

25

When Joseph rejected Potiphar's wife, she accused him of a crime; he went to prison.

26

According to the Gospel of Luke, Mary was a cousin of Elizabeth, who was wife of the priest Zechariah and mother of John the Baptist.

27

The wise woman of Abel of Beth-maacah warned Joab not to attack the city to capture the rebel Sheba. In the end, the citizens gave Joab Sheba's head.

28

When Queen Jezebel decided to have God's prophets murdered, the man in charge of her palace hid a hundred prophets in two caves.

29

Hamutal was the mother of Kings Jehoahaz and Zedekiah, and maybe ruled with them.

50 Winning Facts About WOMEN

30
In the Book of Proverbs, the **Ode to a Capable Wife** lists the duties of women in biblical times, such as rising before dawn to prepare the household.

31
When **Ruth's** husband died, she married his distant relative, as was the custom for widows with no children. This way **the family name was passed down.**

32
Many Marys are in the New Testament: Mary, the mother of Jesus; Mary, the mother of James and Joseph; and Mary Magdelene, Jesus' disciple, are three.

33
Salome, Herodias's daughter, danced beautifully for Herod, so he granted her a wish. For her mother, **she asked for John the Baptist's head**—and got it.

34
The first person Paul converted in Macedonia, today's Greece, was a woman named **Lydia.** She was a merchant who sold purple cloth.

35
From prison, Paul wrote a letter saying that his follower Timothy inherited his sincere faith from his mother, **Eunice,** and his grandmother **Lois.**

36
John the Baptist criticized Herod for marrying **Herodias,** who was already married to Herod's brother.

37
Maacah was a royal princess, and then a queen. But she worshipped gods connected with sorcery and witchcraft, so her son overthrew her.

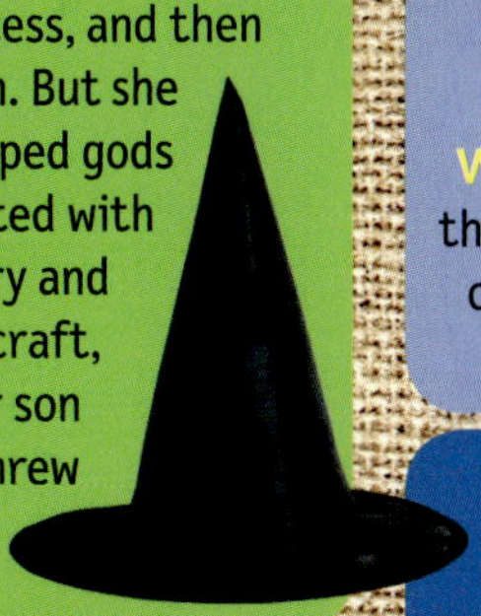

38
When **Martha** complained that her sister, Mary, sat with Jesus instead of helping in the kitchen, Jesus told Martha she **worried about the wrong things.**

39
Moses' sister, **Miriam,** was the **first woman prophet** named in the Bible. After escaping the Egyptians, she and the Israelite women danced.

40
After Nabal insulted David by denying food to his army, **Nabal's clever wife, Abigail,** sent the angry David donkeys carrying bread, fruit, wine, and meat.

41
The childless **Hannah** vowed that if God gave her a son, she would dedicate him to God. When she bore Samuel, she gave him to the priests.

42
As King David lay dying, **Queen Bathsheba** helped their son Solomon become the new king. Solomon respected her wisdom and gave her a throne at his right hand.

43
By marrying King Saul, **Ahinoam** became the first queen of Israel.

44
Risking her life, **Rahab hid Joshua's spies** from the king of Jericho, then lowered them down a rope from her window and told them to hide in the hills.

45
Adah was the first woman, after Eve, to be given **a name.** She was the mother of Jabal, the first tent-dwelling herdsman.

46
Rebekah's nurse, **Deborah,** was so respected that when she died she was buried under an oak tree called Allon-bacuth, **"Oak of Weeping."**

47
When King David danced in the streets to celebrate the Ark of the Covenant coming to Jerusalem, his wife **Michal** scolded him for acting like a fool.

48
Rizpah put on sackcloth and **chased vultures and beasts** from the bodies of her dead sons, who were supposedly killed for their father's offenses.

49
Against God's will, King Saul disguised himself and asked a **woman of Endor** to consult the dead prophet Samuel. Her vision of Samuel terrified Saul.

50
Mary may be the woman in the Book of Revelation at the end of time, "clothed with the sun, with the moon under her feet, and . . . a crown of twelve stars."

15 AMAZING FACTS

❶ **The 12 closest disciples,** or followers, of Jesus were Simon Peter, James, John, Andrew, Philip, Thomas, Bartholomew, Matthew, James (the Lesser), Simon, Thaddaeus, and Judas Iscariot.

❷ How could you tell if a person was an apostle? St. Paul said that **a true apostle** performed his work with utmost "patience, signs and wonders, and mighty works."

❸ **Saul,** who had arrested many of Jesus' followers, became an apostle **after Jesus struck him in a flash of light** and said, "Why do you persecute me?" He also changed his name to Paul.

❹ **Paul had a special mission** as an apostle: to take the Gospel to non-Jews, called Gentiles.

❺ When the disciples went out to spread the Gospel, or word of Jesus, they became known as the Apostles, from the Greek *apostolos*, which means **"one who is sent."**

❻ No one is sure what happened to all the Apostles. Tradition says that **all but one were martyrs,** killed for their religious beliefs; **only John may have lived to a ripe old age.**

❼ The fifth book of the New Testament is called **Acts of the Apostles.** It tells the story of how Christianity—the teachings of Jesus—was spread by his apostles.

❽ **Other apostles** later mentioned in the New Testament include **Barnabas,** Silas, Timothy, Apollos, and Junia.

ABOUT APOSTLES

Stained-glass window showing the Last Supper with Jesus and the Apostles

❾ **The Apostle Paul** is credited with having written nearly half of the books of the New Testament.

❿ When he was arrested for teaching Jesus' words at a Jewish temple, **Paul claimed his right as a Roman citizen to go before a court in Rome.** He may have later died as a martyr, but no one is sure.

⓫ One of the Apostles may have been a **woman.** Paul mentions **Andronicus and Junia,** possibly a female, saying "they were prominent among the apostles."

⓬ **Peter was Jesus' first apostle** and closest friend. His name had been Simon, but Jesus called him Peter, meaning **"rock,"** and told him: "[O]n this rock I will build my church."

⓭ King Herod put the Apostle **Peter** in prison, but **an angel came to the rescue:** Peter's chains fell off, then he followed the angel past the guards and through the city gate as it opened before them.

⓮ The Apostle **Thomas** refused to believe Jesus had risen from the dead until he saw him and touched his wounds. Today a **"doubting Thomas"** is someone who's hard to convince.

⓯ According to the Gospel of Mark, Jesus told his apostles to use the **buddy system.** When he sent them out to spread his message, **he sent them out in pairs.**

GLOSSARY

Ahasuerus King of ancient Persia in the Book of Esther; probably the king known as Xerxes I by historians

Amalekites An ancient people of the Negev who were archenemies of Israel

Amorites An ancient mountain-dwelling people from Syria and Mesopotamia

ancestor A person in someone's family from an earlier time

apostle One who is sent out to spread the word of God. The Twelve Apostles were the main disciples, or students, of Jesus.

Arameans An ancient people who came from Syria. They spoke Aramaic.

Aramaic One of the first languages of the written Bible and the language Jesus probably spoke

Ark of the Covenant A chest containing the tablets on which the Ten Commandments were written

archaeologist Someone who studies the history of the earliest people by examining tools, bones, and other items left behind

Assyrians An ancient people of a mighty kingdom in Mesopotamia, who defeated the northern kingdom of Israel in 722 B.C.E.

Babylonians An ancient people from central-southern Mesopotamia, who besieged Jerusalem and began to deport the Jews in 597 B.C.E.

B.C.E. Meaning "before the Common Era," which is usually used for dates before the birth of Christ

books of the Bible The major sections that make up the Bible, often named after events, people, prophets, kings, or apostles

Canaanites An ancient people living in the area of Israel since the second millennium B.C.E.

C.E. Meaning the "Common Era," which is generally used for dates after the birth of Christ

census The official counting of the number of people in a country

chapters of the Bible The sections that make up each book of the Bible. For instance, the Book of Genesis has 50 chapters.

chariot A carriage pulled by horses and used by warriors in early battles

cherubim A heavenly being. One was put in charge of guarding the gate to Eden after Adam and Eve were turned out.

concubine An unmarried woman who lives with a man and his wife, as if she were another wife

crucifixion The killing of a person by nailing or binding them to a cross

descendant Someone who comes from a particular family

disciple One of the many students of Jesus. The 12 main disciples chosen to spread Jesus' message were called apostles.

exile A period during which a person is forced to live away from home

exodus A situation in which many people leave their home at the same time. For instance, the Israelites made an exodus from Egypt.

frankincense The precious gum resin, a sticky substance, from a tree that grows mainly in Arabia

generation The average length of time between the birth of parents and the birth of their children

Gethsemane The walled garden where Jesus went to pray after the Last Supper, and was later arrested

Gibeonites The people of Gibeon, who descended from the Hivites and Amorites; enemies of the Israelites in the Old Testament

Gospels The first four books of the New Testament

Hittites An ancient people of Anatolia, neighbors of Israel since the time of Abraham

Hivites An ancient people who lived in the mountains of Canaan

icon Images on wood, or paintings, embroidery, or mosaics showing biblical figures such as Jesus, Mary, and angels

idol An image of a false God

incense A substance that is often burned during religious ceremonies and has a pleasant smell

javelin A light spear usually used as a weapon in ancient wars

Jebusites A Canaanite tribe that lived in Jerusalem before King David's conquest

Last Supper Jesus' last meal with his apostles. Afterward Jesus was arrested, then crucified.

leprosy A disease that affects the skin and causes wasting of muscles and deformities

Levite A member of the ancient Israelite tribe of Levi

Mercy Seat The cover of the Ark of the Covenant

Messiah A name given to Jesus as a prophet

Midianites An ancient people who lived in the northwestern region of the Arabian Desert

miracle A surprising event that can't be explained by natural or scientific laws and is often attributed to God's work

monarch The ruler of a territory

mosaic A design, often showing a person or event, made of small pieces of colored glass or tile

myrrh A precious resin used in incense that has a pleasant smell

Nebuchadnezzar King of Neo-Babylonia, who destroyed the temple of Jerusalem and sent the Jews into exile

oasis An area in the desert with a water source, where many plants can grow

offering Something that is given to God as a gift

omen Something that is believed to be a warning about the future

oracle A person who was believed to predict the future, not necessarily through God's inspiration

papyrus A grassy marsh plant that is used for making a paperlike material

patriarch The oldest male head of the family

Perizzites An ancient people who lived in Canaan before the arrival of the Israelites

pharaoh Ruler of ancient Egypt

Phoenicians A seafaring people from Byblos, Sidon, and Tyre, who served as traders during the time of the Old Testament

Philistines An ancient people who lived along the Mediterranean coast near Israel; archenemies of Israel

plague A large number of bothersome and harmful things, such as the plagues God sent to Egypt so Pharaoh would free Moses and the Israelites

poultice A substance that is spread on the skin to heal sores and other injuries

prophet Someone who delivers messages, omens, or warnings that are believed to come from God

quiver A case for carrying arrows

Resurrection The rising of Christ from the dead

Romans People from Rome and Italy. In biblical times they occupied much of the Mediterranean coast.

Sabbath The day of rest and worship, as God intended. Among the Jews, it is celebrated from Friday evening to Saturday evening.

Samaritan A stranger from Samaria, shunned by the people of Israel

scroll Rolled-up paper or leather or parchment, made from sheepskin or goatskin, with writing on it

sulfur A yellow element that has a strong, unpleasant odor

verses of the Bible Short sayings that make up each chapter in the Bible

wadi Dry riverbed that fills with water only during rain

PERSONALITIES

It's hard to pick just a handful of personalities from the thousands of larger-than-life heroes and villains, kings and workers, leaders and lost souls who fill the Bible. Here are a few of the extraordinary men and women you'll meet.

Name: David

Vitals: Introduced in the Book of 1 Samuel, he was the youngest son of Jesse, and a great warrior.

Famous for: Knocking down the giant Goliath with a single stone from his slingshot. David later became king, replacing Saul, who disobeyed God. Despite jealousy and plots of murder against him, David united Israel's 12 tribes into a single nation.

Name: Abraham

Vitals: Introduced in the Book of Genesis; the first patriarch, or forefather, of the Israelites

Famous for: Being so devoted to God as a simple shepherd that he was rewarded with descendants as "numerous as the stars of heaven." This "father of many" gave rise to three of the world's great religions—Judaism, Christianity, and Islam.

Name: Deborah

Vitals: The only female judge of the Israelites mentioned in the Bible. She was also a prophet and a warrior.

Famous for: Successfully leading the Israelites in battle against Jabin, King of Canaan. The Song of Deborah tells of the heroism of Deborah and another strong woman, Jael.

Name: Moses

Vitals: Introduced in Genesis. Born a Hebrew, he was adopted by Pharaoh's daughter and grew up as an Egyptian noble.

Famous for: Freeing the Jews from slavery, leading them out of Egypt, guiding them through the desert for 40 years to the Promised Land, and receiving the Ten Commandments from God at Mount Sinai

Name: Solomon

Vitals: Introduced in the Book of 2 Samuel, Solomon was David and Bathsheba's son.

Famous for: His legendary wisdom, a gift from God. He became king after David, instead of his older brothers, and later built the First Temple to God in Jerusalem. He ended in ruin when he turned to other gods.

FROM THE BIBLE

Name: Jesus

Vitals: Introduced by name in the New Testament: Matthew 1:1. The son of God, born to Mary and Joseph. The four Gospels follow his life.

Famous for: Being the central figure of Christianity as its long-awaited savior, dying on the Cross for humankind's sins, and rising from the dead. His teachings of compassion and forgiveness fill the New Testament.

Name: The Apostles—the original 12 were Simon Peter, James, John, Andrew, Philip, Thomas, Bartholomew, Matthew, James (the Lesser), Simon, Thaddaeus, and Judas Iscariot.

Vitals: Introduced in Matthew, these 12 followers of Jesus were early Christian missionaries, healers, and leaders.

Famous for: Being chosen by Jesus to spread his message. They were given power to cast out evil spirits and heal the sick. Jesus warned that many people would be against them: "I am sending you out like sheep in the midst of wolves . . ."

Name: Mary

Vitals: Introduced by name in the Book of Luke when the angel Gabriel told her she would be the mother of the Messiah, or Jesus

Famous for: Being the mother of Jesus. Mary raised Jesus and became his follower, and then stayed at the foot of the Cross as he died. For Christians, Mary has become the most revered woman in the Bible.

Name: John the Baptist

Vitals: In Luke, the angel Gabriel told John's elderly father that he and his wife would have a son who'd pave the way for the Messiah.

Famous for: Preaching the coming of Jesus, and later baptizing him. John had a large following in the Wilderness of Judea, where he baptized people for the forgiveness of sins. King Herod beheaded John for speaking out against him.

Name: Paul (Roman name), formerly Saul (Jewish name)

Vitals: Introduced in Acts as Saul of Tarsus, a tentmaker. He was committed to destroying anyone who became a Christian.

Famous for: Becoming a Christian when Jesus appeared to him in a bolt of lightning on the road to Damascus. Saul took the name Paul, then spread Christianity to new lands. His writings help make up the New Testament.

Name: Mary Magdalene

Vitals: Introduced in Matthew as witness to Jesus' Crucifixion. Later, in Luke, her story is told from the beginning, when she first met Jesus.

Famous for: Witnessing Jesus' Crucifixion, discovering his empty tomb, and being the first to see him after the Resurrection. Mary Magdalene was one of Jesus' followers, who traveled with him during his days of teaching.

ANNOTATIONS

The entries in *1,000 Facts About the Bible* are based on the New Revised Standard Version of the Bible (NRSV),* widely used by scholars today and recommended by our Board of Advisers. Below are the book, chapter, and verse from the NRSV that relate to most entries. Find the books, websites, and sources for the other entries on the Resources page.

page 12
25 Pint-Size Facts About Children

1. Genesis 4:1–2
2. Genesis 18:12–13
3. Exodus 2:1–10, 15:20
4. Genesis 25:27–28
5. Psalms 127:3–5
6. 1 Samuel 17:34–37
7. 1 Samuel 17:28–49
8. 1 Samuel 17:28–49
9. Jeremiah 1:5
10. Daniel 1
11. Luke 2:49
12. Proverbs 13:22
13. 1 Samuel 18:10–11
14. Matthew 13:55
15. Genesis 37:2–3
16. 2 Kings 5
17. Genesis 22:1–14
18. 1 Timothy
19. 2 Kings 22:1
20. 1 Samuel 1:22
21. Leviticus 20:9
22. 2 Timothy 3:10
23. Matthew 19:14
24. Acts 23:12–35
25. Proverbs 13:24, 23:13–21

page 14
50 Facts About Family Matters

1. Genesis 2:7, 3:20, 4:1–4, 5:30
2. Genesis 4:19
3. Deuteronomy 25:5–10
4. Deuteronomy 21:15–17
5. Deuteronomy 17:17
6. 1 Kings 11:3
7. Psalms 103:17–18
8. Genesis 17:5, 22:17
9. Genesis 16:1–11
10. Genesis 21:1–5
11. Genesis 22:5–12
12. Genesis 25:29–34
13. Genesis 28:5, 29:20
14. Genesis 28:5, 29:16–25
15. Genesis 29:28
16. James 1:27
17. Genesis 49
18. Genesis 37:3, 28
19. Ephesians 6:2
20. Genesis 12:1–6
21. 1 Timothy 5:8
22. Genesis 13:1
23. Psalms 127:3–5
24. Genesis 6:18
25. Genesis 5:27
26. Genesis 10
27. Exodus 2:1–10, 6:16–28, 7:7, 15:20
28. Exodus 6:20
29. Exodus 6:20
30. Exodus 28, 29
31. Joshua 24:15
32. Acts 16:11–15
33. 2 Samuel 16:10–12, 13:23–38
34. Genesis 2:24
35. Proverbs 18:24
36. Genesis 24:1–19
37. Genesis 24:1–67
38. Genesis 26:34–35, 28:7–9
39. Genesis 38
42. Esther 2:7–9
43. 1 Samuel 18:20
44. 2 Samuel 6:23
45. Exodus 20:12
46. Ephesians 6:4
47. Matthew 13:55–56; Mark 6:3
48. Luke 1:35
49. Luke 1:36, 1:60
50. Matthew 1:1–17

page 16
15 Uplifting Facts About Angels

3. Genesis 13:13, 19:1
4. Genesis 18:1–2
5. Genesis 16:11, 14
6. Matthew 22:30; Genesis 6:4
7. Jude 1:5–9; Daniel 10:13–21; Luke 1:19
8. Judges 13:2–24
9. Judges 6:12
10. Matthew 18:10
11. Luke 1:26–38
12. Matthew 2:13
13. Hebrews 13:2
14. Luke 2:10–11
15. Revelation 4:8

page 18
25 Royal and Regal Facts About Kings and Queens

2. 2 Kings 22:1
4. 1 Kings 16:30
5. 2 Kings 25:1–9
6. 1 Samuel 8, 15:22
7. 1 Samuel 15:22, 16:7
8. Matthew 2:1, 2:16–18
9. 1 Kings 10:10
10. 1 Samuel 9:2, 17:45
11. 2 Kings 9:30–37
12. John 19:19–20
13. John 6:15
14. Joshua 12:7–24
16. Joshua 11
17. Matthew 27:29
18. Daniel 5
21. Revelation 19:11–16
22. 1 Kings 12:20; 2 Chronicles 10
24. 1 Kings 16:24
25. Psalms 47:7–8

page 20
15 Luxurious Facts About Palaces

2. 2 Chronicles 4:22; 1 Kings 6:20–21, 30
3. Daniel 4:29
4. 1 Kings 6, 7
5. 2 Samuel 5:11
6. 1 Kings 7:6
7. 2 Samuel 5:11
11. 2 Chronicles 9:18
12. 1 Kings 11
13. Amos 6:4

page 22
15 Flowering Facts About Gardens

1. Proverbs 24:31
2. Genesis 13:10
4. Isaiah 65:2–3
5. Matthew 26:36; John 18:1–12
6. Isaiah 1:8
7. Genesis 9:20; Leviticus 23:22
8. Genesis 2:8
9. 1 Kings 21:8–14
10. John 19:41; Luke 23:33
11. 2 Kings 21:18
12. Amos 9:14
13. Esther 1:4–8
14. Genesis 3:24
15. 2 Kings 25:4; Nehemiah 3:15; John 9:7

page 24
25 Beastly Facts About Animals

1. Job 41:1–26
2. Acts 12:23
3. Mark 10:25
4. Numbers 23:22, 24:8; Job 39:9; Psalms 22:21, 29:6, 92:10; Deuteronomy 33:17; Isaiah 34:7
5. Zechariah 9:9; Matthew 21:7
6. Job 42:12
7. Revelation 6:7
8. Leviticus 1:1–17
9. Luke 8:26–39
10. Genesis 24:10–63
11. Exodus 19:12–14; Psalms 81:2–4
12. Job 40:15–20
13. Numbers 22:28
14. 1 Kings 10:22
15. Psalms 63:10
16. 1 Kings 10:26
17. Daniel 6
18. Revelation 12:1–5
19. 2 Kings 2:23–25
20. Deuteronomy 21:1–9
21. Numbers 11:31
22. Genesis 3
23. Exodus 36:14
24. Proverbs 6:6
25. Isaiah 40:31; Deuteronomy 32:11–12

page 26
15 Bouncing Biblical Baby Facts

1. 1 Kings 3:16–28
2. Genesis 25:26
3. Matthew 2:16–18
4. Ezekiel 16:4
5. Luke 2:1–20
6. Luke 2:22–39
8. Luke 2:22–24; Leviticus 12:2–8
9. 1 Samuel 1:19–25
10. Ruth 4:15–17
11. Genesis 35:18
12. Genesis 21:8
13. Psalms 127:3–5
14. 1 Samuel 1:11
15. Matthew 21:15–16

page 28
75 Facts About Laws and Commandments

7. Exodus 20:1–17; Deuteronomy 5:6–21
8. Exodus 20:1–17
9. Exodus 25:10–20
10. Exodus 26:1–37, 38:21–30
11. Exodus 13–17
15. Genesis 2:16, 9:4–7
16. Exodus 18:13–26
17. Exodus 20:10
18. Exodus 22:25–26
19. Exodus 23:11
20. Exodus 23:15
21. Exodus 34:1
22. Leviticus 11
23. Leviticus 11:20–23
24. Leviticus 14:34–42
25. Leviticus 15:5
26. Leviticus 16:30–34
27. Leviticus 19:9–10
28. Leviticus 19:18; Luke 23:34
29. Leviticus 19:26
30. Leviticus 19:27
31. Leviticus 19:19, 19:28
32. Leviticus 19:28
33. Leviticus 20:27
34. Leviticus 21:5, 10
35. Leviticus 25:26–31
36. Deuteronomy 12:23
37. Deuteronomy 17:14–20
38. Deuteronomy 19:15
39. Deuteronomy 20:3
40. Deuteronomy 20:19–20
41. Deuteronomy 22:10
42. Deuteronomy 22:6–7
43. Deuteronomy 22:8
44. Deuteronomy 23:13
45. Deuteronomy 23:24–25
46. Deuteronomy 25:4
47. Judges
48. Numbers 6:1–5
49. Ruth 4:7
50. Exodus 22:21; Hebrews 13:2
51. James 4:12
52. 1 Kings 22:34–36
53. Psalms 19:7–10
54. Proverbs 25:16
55. Proverbs 14:31, 29:7; Psalms 82:1–4
56. Daniel 6:8
57. Leviticus 2:13; Ezekiel 43:24
58. Exodus 20:4
59. Matthew 6:1
60. Matthew 7:12; Luke 6:31
61. Matthew 7:15
62. Matthew 7:7; Luke 6:30
63. Matthew 17:24
64. Matthew 22:37–40
65. Matthew 26:63
66. Matthew 5:38–48; Luke 6:29
67. Romans 12:14
68. Matthew 10:16; 1 Corinthians 15:58
69. Deuteronomy 15:7–8; Proverbs 3:27
70. 2 Corinthians 8
71. Ephesians 5:18; 2 Corinthians 6:14–18
72. Ephesians 4:29
73. Philippians 2:14
74. 1 Thessalonians 5:14
75. 1 Timothy 6:18

page 30
25 Painful Facts About Punishments

1. John 19
2. Exodus 21:28–32; Leviticus 24:16
3. Acts 16:22
4. Mark 15:15
5. 2 Thessalonians 1:5–9
6. Daniel 5:1–30
7. Acts 12:20–23
8. Genesis 19:26
9. 2 Samuel 6:7
10. Revelation 9:5–12
11. Genesis 6
12. Ezekiel 22:20–22
13. Exodus 1:11
14. Exodus 32:20–28
15. Numbers 15:32–36
16. Genesis 3:14
17. Joshua 7:1–26
18. Acts 5:1–11
19. Judges 9:52–57
20. 2 Kings 5
21. 1 Samuel 11:2
22. Exodus 21:24
23. 1 Samuel 5
24. Judges 1:5–7
25. Revelation 21:8

page 32
15 Trendy Facts About Clothing to Try On

1. Micah 1:8
2. Matthew 22:11–12
3. Jeremiah 13:1; Deuteronomy 22:12, 24:13; Ruth 13:5
4. John 19:23
5. Isaiah 3:22–23
6. Deuteronomy 22:11
7. Numbers 15:37
8. Exodus 22:26–27
9. Genesis 3:7
10. Exodus 28:6–21
11. Genesis 37:3
12. Genesis 24:65
13. Isaiah 3:24; Ezekiel 16:10
14. Acts 12:8
15. Ezekiel 16:10

page 34
15 Long and Short Facts About Hair

1. Genesis 25:25
2. 2 Kings 1:8
3. Judges 16:19
4. 2 Samuel 14:26
5. Daniel 4:20–33
6. Numbers 6:5
7. Ezra 9
8. Job 1:20
9. Ezekiel 5:1–2
10. Matthew 10:30
11. 1 Corinthians 11:14–15
12. Solomon 4:1
13. 2 Samuel 18:9
14. Isaiah 7:20
15. John 12:1–6

page 36
15 Facts About Weapons That Will Have You Up in Arms

1. 1 Samuel 17:4–7, 45
2. Isaiah 2:3–4
3. Genesis 3:24
4. 1 Samuel 17:34–50
5. John 18:10–11
6. Hebrews 4:12; Revelation 19:15
7. 1 Samuel 18:11
8. Judges 4
10. Isaiah 14:19; Ezekiel 26:11
11. Genesis 4:8
12. Genesis 27:3
13. Psalms 44:6–7
14. 1 Samuel 17:40; Psalms 23:4
15. Ecclesiastes 9:18

page 38
25 Fighting Facts About Battles

1. Joshua 6
2. 1 Samuel 17
3. Exodus 14:14; Deuteronomy 20:1, 4; 2 Chronicles 13:12
4. Joshua 10:31
5. Deuteronomy 20:10
6. 2 Kings 24:7–20
7. 2 Kings 19:11
8. Psalms 68:30
9. Deuteronomy 20:7; 24:5
10. Numbers 13, 21; Joshua 2, 7
11. Numbers 10, 31; Joshua 6; Judges 7
12. 1 Chronicles 26:27
13. Joshua 7:1–12
14. Exodus 17:8–15
15. Isaiah 2:4
16. Revelation 16:14
17. 2 Chronicles 20:21–23
18. Judges 7
19. Numbers 21:34
20. 2 Kings 7:6–7
21. Judges 15:14–15
22. 1 Samuel 4:1–11
23. 1 Chronicles 10:1–4
24. Deuteronomy 1:41–46
25. 2 Kings 19:34–35

page 40
25 Blooming Facts About Plants and Flowers

3. Genesis 3:7
4. Isaiah 38:21
5. Genesis 1:11–12
6. Matthew 2:11; Exodus 30:34–38
7. 2 Samuel 5:11; 1 Chronicles 17:1; 2 Chronicles 2:3–8
8. Matthew 6:25–34
9. Matthew 21:1–8
10. John 15:1–4
12. Exodus 25:10
13. Exodus 15:27
14. Deuteronomy 8:8
15. Genesis 43:11
16. Revelation 22:2
17. 2 Samuel 5:23–25
18. Exodus 2:1–7
19. Exodus 12:8
20. Leviticus 14:4
21. Numbers 11:5
22. Matthew 27:29
23. Jonah 4:5–6
24. 2 Samuel 17:28
25. Exodus 30:23

page 42
50 Facts About Miracles

1. Genesis 1–2
3. Genesis 6:5–18
4. Genesis 11:1–9
5. Acts 5:15–16
6. Exodus 7–12
7. Exodus 14:21–15:21
8. Joshua 10:12–14
9. 2 Kings 2:11
10. Daniel 6
11. Hebrews 7:3
12. Daniel 3
13. Jonah 1–17
14. Daniel 5
15. Exodus 3:2
16. Exodus 4:1–10
17. Exodus 16:1–36
18. 2 Kings 5
19. John 1:14
20. Matthew 2:1–9
21. John 2
22. Luke 5:1–11
23. Mark 1:40–45
24. Matthew 8:23–27
25. Mark 5:1–20
26. Mark 5:21–43
27. Matthew 9:32–34
28. John 5:1–18
29. Matthew 14:13–21
30. Matthew 14:29
31. Matthew 17:24–27
32. Luke 17:11–19
33. Luke 14:1–6
34. John 11:11–44
35. Matthew 20:29–34
36. Luke 22:49–51
37. Matthew 17:14–20
38. Luke 24:1–53
39. John 21:25
40. Genesis 19:24
41. Exodus 15:19–20
42. Exodus 19:18
43. Exodus 13:21
44. 1 Kings 17:6
45. 2 Kings 1:9–12
46. 1 Kings 13:4–6
47. 2 Kings 2:14
48. Joshua 3:7–17
49. Luke 1:26–39
50. Acts 1:9

page 44
25 Temples and Temple Artifact Facts

1. Exodus 36:8–38
2. Exodus 38
3. Numbers 10:1–10
4. Exodus 37–38; Leviticus 24:5
6. Exodus 27; Leviticus 24:1–4
7. Exodus 30:34–38, 37
8. Exodus 37:1–9
9. Exodus 25:16
11. Exodus 25:17–21
13. Matthew 27:51
14. 1 Chronicles 22:2–5; 1 Kings 6:1–22
16. Ezra 3:8–13
17. 2 Chronicles 12:1–11
19. Acts 3:1–8
21. 1 Kings 6:1–22
22. Matthew 21:12
25. 1 Kings 7:1–10

page 46
75 Hard-Working Facts About Jobs

1. 2 Samuel 5:11
2. Matthew 13:55
3. Luke 2:1–3
4. Luke 2:8–20
5. Exodus 3:1
6. Genesis 4:20
7. Genesis 4:22
8. Luke 19
9. Luke 19:2 (King James Version)
10. Luke 18:9–14
11. Matthew 9:9
12. 2 Timothy 4:14
13. Genesis 40:5
14. Nehemiah 1:11
15. 1 Samuel 9:23–24
16. Matthew 24:41
17. Matthew 4:18
18. Genesis 4:20–22
19. Genesis 35:8
20. Genesis 10:9
21. Genesis 4:2–4
22. Genesis 4:3–4
23. Judges 2:16
24. 1 Samuel 8:5
25. Genesis 42:6

26. Daniel 6:2
27. Acts 16:23
28. Ezra 7:8–10
29. 2 Samuel 8:16–18
30. 1 Kings 4:1–19
31. 1 Kings 4:1–19
32. Joshua 9:21–23
33. Nehemiah 3:8
34. Acts 19–24
35. 1 Samuel 13:19–22
36. Genesis 2:7; Romans 9:21; Job 10:9
37. Acts 9:43
38. Acts 18:3
39. Malachi 3:2
40. Luke 10:35
41. 1 Chronicles 7
42. Isaiah 55:4
43. Psalms 68:24–26
44. 1 Kings 3:16–28
45. Acts 13:7
46. Genesis 9:20; 2 Chronicles 26:10
47. Ezekiel 27:12–24
48. 1 Kings 10:26
49. Acts 8:26–27
50. Colossians 4:14
51. John 18:1–12
52. 1 Samuel 16:21–2
53. Matthew 26:57
54. Leviticus 21:11, 5
55. Ezekiel 33:3–4
56. Matthew 8:9
57. Deuteronomy 18:18
58. Amos 7:14
59. Numbers 18:2
60. Revelation 1:5–6
61. 1 Timothy 3:2
62. Ephesians 4:11
63. Isaiah 14:8
64. Isaiah 24:1
65. Deuteronomy 23:20
66. Numbers 6:1–21; Judges 13:5
67. Exodus 1:19
68. 1 Timothy 5:18
69. Isaiah 47:13
70. Genesis 11:3
71. 2 Chronicles 30:6
72. Genesis 42:23
73. 2 Kings 12:12
74. Genesis 43:16
75. Acts 17:18

page 48
25 Telling Facts About Prophets

1. 1 Kings 18:4; Isaiah 30:10
2. 1 Kings 22
3. Genesis 20:4–6
4. Isaiah 20:2–3
6. Deuteronomy 34:10
7. Acts 2:14–17
8. Judges 4:4; Micah 6:4; 2 Kings 22:14; Nehemiah 6:14
9. Isaiah 19:5
10. Deuteronomy 18:18
12. Jonah 2:2
14. Isaiah 13:19
15. Exodus 2:5–10; 1 Kings 19:15–21; Amos 1:1
17. 1 Kings 19:10; 2 Kings 2:11
18. Ezekiel 37:1–14
19. Jeremiah 9:1
20. Matthew 21:26; Luke 7:28
21. 2 Peter 1:21
22. Judges 4–5
23. Deuteronomy 13:1–5
24. Matthew 25:32–46; Revelation 1–7; Thessalonians 4:16–17
25. 1 Samuel 3, 10:1, 16:1–3

page 50
15 Routine Facts About Daily Life

1. Genesis 24:10–26
2. Exodus 16
3. Matthew 25:1–9
4. Isaiah 38:12; Luke 2:8–12
5. 2 Samuel 18:24
6. Leviticus 23:39–43
7. Genesis 43:33; 1 Samuel 20:5, 18
8. John 5:8
9. Revelation 3:8
10. Genesis 11:3
11. 1 Samuel 9:26
12. Isaiah 5:2; Proverbs 18:10
13. Isaiah 38:12; Matthew 6:28
14. Jeremiah 32:13–14
15. Matthew 26:23; Mark 14:20

page 52
15 Glittering Facts About Fashion

1. Genesis 41:42
2. Numbers 31:50
3. 2 Kings 9:30–35
4. Matthew 7:6
5. Genesis 35:1–4
7. Jeremiah 22:24; Genesis 41:41–42
8. Isaiah 3:18–20
9. Esther 2:12
10. Song of Solomon 1:10
11. Genesis 24:20–30
12. Exodus 38:8
13. Mark 14:3–5
14. Deuteronomy 6:6–8
15. Ecclesiastes 9:8–9

page 54
25 Harmonious Facts About Music and Poetry

1. Exodus 15:20–21
2. 1 Samuel 10:1–5
3. Ephesians 5:19
4. Psalms, Proverbs, Song of Solomon
5. 2 Chronicles 5:11–14
6. Psalms 33
7. Luke 1:45–55
8. Psalms 98:5
9. Psalms 27:1–2
10. Genesis 3:22
12. Psalms 103
14. 1 Chronicles 15:27–28
15. Ezekiel 33:32
16. 1 Chronicles 15:16–24
17. Daniel 3:10–20
18. Judges 5:3
19. Acts 16:25
21. Ephesians 5:19
22. 1 Samuel 16:23
23. Matthew 26:30
24. Job 38:7
25. Genesis 37:3–4

page 56
35 Sickening Facts About Plagues and Diseases

1. Exodus 7–11
2. Exodus 8:1–15
3. Exodus 8:20–24
4. Exodus 10:1–6
5. Exodus 11:1–8
6. Exodus 30:12
7. Exodus 32:34–35
8. Leviticus 26:20–22
9. Revelation 8:2–13, 11:19, 15:1–21
10. Numbers 16:48–50
11. Deuteronomy 28:27
12. Deuteronomy 28:34
13. Leviticus 26:14–16
14. Luke 14:2
15. 2 Chronicles 21:10–20
16. Matthew 17:15
17. Deuteronomy 28:22
18. Mark 5:1–5
19. Luke 17:12
20. Deuteronomy 28:22
21. Numbers 12:10–14
22. Ezekiel 30:21
23. Leviticus 13
24. 2 Chronicles 16:10–14
25. Colossians 4:14; Matthew 10:1
26. Numbers 21:7
27. Matthew 12:24–30
28. Mark 10:46
29. Jeremiah 8:22
30. 2 Kings 20:7
31. John 5:1–10
32. Leviticus 15:28–30
33. Mark 5:27–29
34. John 19:40
35. Proverbs 17:22

page 58
15 Revealing Facts About Dreams and Visions

1. Genesis 28:10–15, 46:1–7
2. Exodus 24:9–12
3. Zechariah 1:7–11
4. Exodus 33:20–23
5. Ezekiel 10:9–14
6. Luke 1:26–56
7. Matthew 28:1–6
8. Acts 9:1–19
9. Isaiah 6:1–7
10. Daniel 7:7–8
11. Revelation 1:14–16
12. Revelation 4:7–8
13. Revelation 8:2–19, 15:1
14. Revelation 12:1–9
15. Revelation 21:9–11

page 60
15 Building Facts of the Biblical World

1. Joshua 4:9
2. 2 Chronicles 26:9
3. Genesis 11:4
4. Jeremiah 51:58
5. 1 Kings 6; 2 Chronicles 3:1
6. Acts 19:34–35
8. Joshua 6:20
12. Acts 10
13. Ezra 5:13–16
14. Joshua 11:10
15. Genesis 23:1–10

page 62
15 Facts About Noah and His Awesome Ark

1. Genesis 7:6
2. Genesis 6:14
4. Genesis 6:16
5. Genesis 6:15
8. Genesis 6:19–20
9. Genesis 7:13
10. Genesis 7:12
12. Genesis 8:8–13
13. Genesis 8:17
15. Genesis 9:28–29

page 64
15 Mouthwatering Facts About Food

1. Exodus 16:31
2. Numbers 11:5
3. Deuteronomy 8:8
4. 1 Chronicles 16:3
5. Numbers 17:8
6. Nehemiah 13:15–16
7. Leviticus 19:10; Ruth 2
8. Genesis 43:11
9. Numbers 20:5
10. Leviticus 11
11. John 6:35
12. Genesis 27:6–20
13. Matthew 14:13–20; John 6:1–14
14. Psalms 104:14
15. Luke 15:18–24

page 66
35 Facts About Trade and Money That You Can Bank On

2. 2 Kings 7:1
3. Genesis 23:16
4. Genesis 23:16, 24:22
5. Exodus 25:39, 38:26; 1 Kings 10:17; Leviticus 27:25; 1 Samuel 13:21 (New King James Version); Job 42:11
7. 1 Chronicles 22:14
8. 1 Kings 10:14
9. 1 Samuel 9:8
12. Matthew 22:19
13. Mark 12:16; Luke 20:24
14. 1 Kings 10:28–29
16. John 2:14
17. Mark 11:15
18. Deuteronomy 23:20
19. Matthew 21:12
20. Judges 16:5
21. Genesis 23:15
22. Genesis 37:25–28
25. Matthew 26:14–16
26. 1 Timothy 6:10
27. Isaiah 23:1–10
29. 2 Samuel 12:30
31. Luke 12:33–34
32. Numbers 21:22–23
33. Luke 10:30–37
35. Matthew 17:27

page 68
15 Refreshing Facts About Bodies of Water

1. Isaiah 41:18
2. Daniel 10:4–6
3. Luke 5:1
4. Exodus 7:20
5. Genesis 15:18
6. 1 Kings 17:1–10
7. Exodus 2:3
8. Genesis 13:8–10
9. Genesis 16:7–11
10. Genesis 2:10–14
11. Mark 1:4–5
12. Exodus 15:27
13. Revelation 20:10
14. Matthew 8:28–32
15. Genesis 41:1–30

page 70
15 Blistering Facts About the Desert

1. Genesis 21:21; Exodus 19:1; Numbers 10:12
2. Deuteronomy 8:2
3. Exodus 15:22
4. Numbers 20:1
5. Numbers 20:11
6. Genesis 21:14
7. Genesis 21:20–21
8. 1 Samuel 24:1–3
9. Psalms 107:35; Isaiah 35:6, 43:20
11. Mark 1:4
12. Proverbs 21:19
13. Judges 5
14. Matthew 4:1–11
15. Exodus 16:1

page 72
15 Inspirational Facts About Biblical Art

3. Inspired by Matthew 26:25–27, 46–49
4. Inspired by Judges 15:3–5
5. Inspired by Luke 23:26–43
6. Inspired by Genesis
8. Inspired by John 19:25–37
9. Inspired by Luke 10:25–37
10. Inspired by Genesis 49:28
11. Inspired by Matthew 26:25–27
12. Inspired by Exodus 2:1–25
13. Inspired by Matthew
15. Inspired by Matthew 26:20–29

page 74
25 Facts About Bible Expressions

1. Leviticus 16:20–22
2. Isaiah 11:12
3. 1 Corinthians 15:52
4. John 20:24–29
5. Daniel 5
6. Isaiah 40:15
7. Job 19:20
8. Psalms 8:2
9. Deuteronomy 32:10; Zechariah 2:8
10. Matthew 5:38; Exodus 21:24
11. Matthew 7:15
12. Ecclesiastes 10:1
13. Jeremiah 13:23
14. Job 15:7
15. Psalms 107:27
16. Psalms 72:9
17. Ecclesiastes 9:4
18. Genesis 2:15–17
19. Genesis 3:3
20. Ecclesiastes 8:15
21. Acts 13:22
22. 1 Timothy 6:12
23. Psalms 51:7
24. John 8:7
25. Luke 10:30–37

page 76
15 Tongue-Twisting Facts About Biblical Words

1. 2 Chronicles 20
2. Isaiah, Zephaniah, Obadiah, Habakkuk
3. Isaiah 8:3
4. Exodus 4:10
5. Ezra 2:29; Isaiah 46:1
6. Genesis 41:45
7. Luke 1:20
8. Genesis 11:7–9
9. Daniel 5:25–26
10. 1 Esdras 6:20; Haggai 2:21
11. 2 Samuel 4:4
12. Mark 7:33
13. Daniel 1:7
14. Daniel 1:3–7
15. Luke 11:15

page 78
50 Fabulous Facts About Numbers and Figures

1. Numbers 1:1–5
2. Numbers 1:26–27
3. Matthew 1:17
4. Revelation 21:17; Exodus 25:24–25
5. Exodus 25:24–25
6. 1 Kings 6:2
7. 1 Kings 11:3
9. 1 Kings 4:32; Proverbs 11:22
10. Ezekiel 45:11–14; Leviticus 14:15
11. Exodus 39:1
13. Numbers 1:46
14. Exodus 26:1–2
15. Genesis 6:15
16. Judges 12:8–9
17. Psalms
21. Genesis 5:27
22. NRSV
23. NRSV
24. 2 Chronicles 2:2
25. Revelation 6:1–8
27. Genesis 1:16; Exodus 25:22; Luke 10:1
28. Ecclesiastes 4:9
30. Revelation 13:18
31. 1 Corinthians 15:4
32. Luke 22:54–62
33. Daniel 7
34. 1 Corinthians 13:13
35. Revelation 9:16–17
36. Genesis 2:10–14
37. Matthew 14:13–21
38. Matthew 27:3–5
39. Jonah 1:17
41. Genesis 2:2–3
42. Exodus 25:31–40
43. Genesis 41:1–36
44. Matthew 18:22
45. Psalms 12:6
46. Galatians 5:22–23
47. Luke 8:2
48. 1 Kings 11:30–35
49. Revelation 21:12
50. Revelation 12:1–3

page 80
25 Moving Facts About Journeys

1. Genesis 11:31
2. Matthew 2:1
3. Luke 2:1–7
4. Genesis 14:12–15
5. Genesis 22:1–19
6. Luke 2:1–7; Matthew 2:1–15
7. Luke 1:26–42
8. Nehemiah 1:1–2:20
9. 1 Samuel 9:3–30, 10:1
10. Judges 4:4–24
11. 1 Samuel 4:1–7
12. 1 Samuel 17:1–58
13. Ruth 1:1–19
14. Ezekiel 27
15. 2 Corinthians 11:26
16. Numbers 31
17. Esther 8
18. 2 Corinthians 11:25–26
19. Luke 2:41
20. Exodus 23:14–17; Judges 21:19
21. Genesis 37:25
22. Acts 13:13–52
23. Acts 16:25–35
24. Matthew 4:13
25. Numbers 20:14–21

page 82
25 Villainous Facts and Dastardly Deeds

1. Acts 23:12
2. Genesis 3:2–4
3. Genesis 31:19–35
4. 1 Samuel 18:17
5. Genesis 25:34
6. Esther 3
7. Genesis 4:1–8
8. Matthew 27:24
9. Acts 7:54–60, 8:1–3
10. 2 Samuel 4:5–7
11. Job 1–2:3
12. 2 Samuel 15:2–17
13. Exodus 5
14. John 19:28–30
15. Judges 9:1–5
16. Luke 16:19–21
17. 1 Kings 3:16–28
18. 2 Chronicles 22:10–12
19. 2 Samuel 20:10
20. Genesis 37:19–32
21. Acts 7:18–19
22. 2 Samuel 11:1–20
23. Luke 22:64
24. Matthew 26:15, 47–50
25. Genesis 18:22–33

page 84
50 Winning Facts About Women

1. Judges 4:4–5
2. Judges 4:10
3. Judith 8:7, 13:6–10
4. Judith 8:11–14
5. Luke 1:26–38
6. Luke 1:42
7. Luke 8:2–3
8. 1 Kings 11:9–14
9. Judges 4:21
10. Esther 4:11–16
11. 1 Kings 10:1–13
12. Genesis 16:11–14
13. Exodus 1:15–21
14. Exodus 2:5–10
15. Ruth 1:16, 4:17
16. Luke 2:36–38
17. 2 Chronicles 22:10–12
18. 2 Samuel 14
19. Judges 16
20. Genesis 3:6
21. Acts 18:18, 24–26; Romans 16:3–4
22. Acts 9:40
23. John 19:25–27
24. John 20:10–18
25. Genesis 39:1–20
26. Luke 1:39–44
27. 2 Samuel 20:16–22
28. 1 Kings 18:3–5
29. 2 Kings 23:30–32, 24:17–19
30. Proverbs 31:10–31
31. Deuteronomy 25:5–10; Ruth 4:10
32. Luke 1:26–28; Matthew 27:55–61; Luke 8:2
33. Mark 6:14–29; Matthew 14:1–12
34. Acts 16:11–15
35. 2 Timothy 1:5
36. Matthew 14:1–11; Mark 6:14–28; Luke 3:19
37. 1 Kings 15:13
38. Luke 10:38–42; John 11:1–45
39. Exodus 15:20
40. 1 Samuel 25:18–25
41. 1 Samuel 1:28, 2:1–10, 19–21
42. 1 Kings 1:28–31
43. 1 Samuel 14:50
44. Joshua 2:1–24
45. Genesis 4.19–22
46. Genesis 35:8
47. 2 Samuel 6:14–23
48. 2 Samuel 3:7; 21:8–15
49. 1 Samuel 28:3–25
50. Revelation 12:1–5

page 86
15 Amazing Facts About Apostles

1. Matthew 10:2–4
2. 2 Corinthians 12:12
3. Acts 9:1–19
4. Ephesians 3:1–2
5. Acts 1:8
7. Acts 14:14; 1 Thessalonians 1:1, 2:6; 1 Corinthians 4:9; Roman 16:7
8. Acts
10. Acts 22:25–29
11. Romans 16:7
12. Matthew 16:18–19
13. Acts 12:7–11
14. John 20:24–29
15. Mark 6:7

INDEX

Boldface indicates illustrations.

RESOURCES

To learn more about the people, places, events, and archaeology of the biblical world, look into these sources:

Books:

Bowker, John. *The Complete Bible Handbook.* DK Publishing, 2001.

Cline, Eric. *From Eden to Exile: Unraveling Mysteries of the Bible.* National Geographic Society, 2008.

Collins, Michael, editor. *The Illustrated Bible Story by Story.* DK Publishing, 2012.

Currie, Robin, and Stephen Hyslop. *The Letter and the Scroll: What Archaeology Tells Us About the Bible.* National Geographic Society, 2009.

Derson, Denise: *What Life Was Like on the Banks of the Nile.* Time-Life Education, 1997.

Esposito, John, and Susan Tyler Hitchcock. *Geography of Religion.* National Geographic Society, 2006.

Fischer, Jean, and Tracy M. Sumner. *Big Bible Guide: Kids' Bible Dictionary & Handbook.* Barbour Publishing, Inc., 2013.

Geoghegan, Jeffrey, and Michael Homan. *The Bible for Dummies.* John Wiley & Sons, Inc., 2003.

Isbouts, Jean-Pierre. *The Biblical World: An Illustrated Atlas.* National Geographic Society, 2007.

Isbouts, Jean-Pierre. *Who's Who in the Bible: Unforgettable People and Timeless Stories From Genesis to Revelation.* National Geographic Society, 2013.

Lloyd-Jones, Sally. *The Jesus Storybook Bible.* Zondervan Publishing, 2007.

Miller, Stephen M. *The Complete Guide to the Bible.* Barbour Publishing, Inc., 2007.

Schneider, Tammi J. *Mothers of Promise: Women in the Book of Genesis.* Baker Academic, 2008.

Websites

www.BibleGateway.com (NRSV)*
www.bible-history.com
www.biblehub.com
www.bible.org
www.bibleplaces.com
www.bibleresources.americanbible.org
www.biblicalarchaeology.org
www.jewishvirtuallibrary.org
www.thekingsbible.com
www.oxfordbiblicalstudies.com
www.StudyLight.org

CREDITS

Abbreviation: SS=Shutterstock

Cover: (Garden of Eden), Robert Harding Picture Library Ltd/Alamy; (Tower of Babel), Image Asset Management Ltd./Alamy; (wafers & wine), Mk74/Dreamstime.com; (lion), Eric Isselee/SS; (10 commandments), jsp/SS; (church), kristina-s/iStockphoto; (dove), Tischenko Irina/SS; (nativity), D. Hurst/Alamy; (stained glass), Alan Harden/Alamy; (fish), kristina-s/iStockphoto; (blue cross background), Charon/Dreamstime.com; (stained glass), Alan Harden/Alamy; (yellow background), Attitude/SS; **Back Cover:** (apple), blackred/iStockphoto; (sheep), Eric Isselee/SS; (Mary and baby Jesus), Musée Bonnat, Bayonne, France/The Bridgeman Art Library; (Star of David), cl2004lhy/SS; **Spine:** (stained glass), Alan Harden/Alamy; 1, The Granger Collection, NYC; 3, IOSIF CHEZAN/SS; 4-5, Peter Adams/The Image Bank/Getty Images; 5 (UP CTR), Tischenko Irina/SS; 5 (LO LE), Mega Pixel/SS; 5 (UP RT), George Dukinas/SS; 5 (LO RT), The Granger Collection, NYC; 5 (UP CTR), Moment Open/Getty Images; 5 (LO CTR), The Print Collector/Alamy; 6, North Wind Picture Archives/Alamy; 8 (LO CTR), Awe Inspiring Images/SS; 8-9, S_Photo/SS; 8 (UP CTR), INTERFOTO/Alamy; 8 (UP RT), jvphoto/Alamy; 9 (UP LE), SmileStudio/SS; 9 (LO CTR), Mary Evans Picture Library/Alamy; 9 (UP RT), amana images inc./Alamy; 9 (CTR RT), Just2shutter/SS; 10 (UP RT), alexsol/SS; 10 (LO CTR), Heritage Image Partnership Ltd./Alamy; 10 (CTR LE), www.BibleLandPictures.com/Alamy; 10 (UP CTR), PARIS PIERCE/Alamy; 10 (LO LE), Seleznev Oleg/SS; 10 (LO CTR), Heritage Image Partnership Ltd./Alamy; 11 (UP LE), Alexander Hoffmann/SS; 11 (LO CTR), Zvonimir Atletic/SS; 11 (UP CTR), Ashwin/SS; 11 (LO LE), Aron Brand/SS; 11 (LO CTR), The Print Collector/SS; 11 (LO RT), wjarek/SS; 11 (UP LE), Francesco Bencivenga/SS; 11 (CTR RT), Art Directors & TRIP/Alamy; 12 (LO CTR), Ivonne Wierink/SS; 12 (UP LE), Lebrecht Music and Arts Photo Library/Alamy; 12 (UP CTR), Dragance137/SS; 12 (LO LE), Mary Evans Picture Library/Alamy; 12 (LO CTR), Art Directors & TRIP /Alamy; 13 (CTR RT), Eric Isselee/SS; 13 (UP LE), Look and Learn/The Bridgeman Art Library; 13 (UP RT), Look and Learn/The Bridgeman Art Library; 13 (LO LE), Look and Learn/The Bridgeman Art Library; 13 (LO RT), Lebrecht Music and Arts Photo Library/Alamy; 14 (CTR), Just2shutter/SS; 14 (CTR), billdayone/SS; 14 (UP LE), De Agostini Picture Library/Gianni Dagli Orti/The Bridgeman Art Library; 14 (UP RT), De Agostini Picture Library/The Bridgeman Art Library; 14 (CTR), IgorGolovniov/SS; 14 (LO LE), Gemenacom/SS; 14 (LO LE), Galina Gutarin/SS; 14-15 (background), Donjiy/SS; 15 (UP CTR), VERSUSstudio/SS; 15 (CTR), Carol Mellema/SS; 15 (UP RT), Zvonimir Atletic/SS; 15 (LO LE), Elnur/SS; 15 (LO LE), albund/SS; 15 (LO RT), De Jongh Photography/SS; 16 (UP LE), The Bridgeman Art Library; 16-17, Detroit Institute of Arts, USA; Bequest of Eleanor Clay Ford/The Bridgeman Art Library; 16 (CTR RT), Founders Society Purchase, R.H. Tannahill Foundation fund/The Bridgeman Art Library; 16 (LO LE), FineArt/Alamy; 17 (CTR RT), Renata Sedmakova/SS; 17 (UP RT), jozef sedmak/Alamy; 17 (UP LE), Giraudon/The Bridgeman Art Library; 17 (LO RT), Giraudon/The Bridgeman Art Library; 18 (UP RT), Gautier22/SS; 18, Furtseff/SS; 18 (LO LE), Vlue/SS; 18 (CTR LE), Robert Harding Picture Library Ltd/Alamy; 18 (LO CTR), Art Directors & TRIP/Alamy; 19 (CTR RT), albund/SS; 19 (CTR RT), Stocksnapper/SS; 19 (UP LE), The Granger Collection, NYC; 19 (LO RT), www.BibleLandPictures.com/Alamy; 20 (UP LE), Madlen/SS; 20-21, HIP/Art Resource; 20 (CTR RT), North Wind Picture Archives/Alamy; 20 (LO LE), Hanan Isachar/Alamy; 21 (UP RT), Carlos Caetano/SS; 21 (CTR RT), Voronin76/SS; 21 (UP LE), Gabi Laron/The Hebrew University of Jerusalem; 21 (LO LE), Erich Lessing/Art Resource, NY; 22 (UP RT), Jeanie333/SS; 22 (CTR LE), Dulce Rubia/SS; 22 (CTR RT), Todd Bolen/BiblePlaces.com; 22 (LO LE), Cameraphoto Arte Venezia/The Bridgeman Art Library; 22-23, Victoria & Albert Museum, London, UK/The Bridgeman Art Library; 23 (UP RT), SeDmi/SS; 23 (CTR LE), Thomas R. Fletcher/Alamy; 23 (CTR RT), Ninell/SS; 23 (LO RT), IOSIF CHEZAN/SS; 24 (UP LE), Algol/SS; 24 (UP LE), Catmando/SS; 24 (UP CTR), Chronicle/Alamy; 24 (UP RT), Vladyslav Danilin/SS; 24 (CTR LE), Eric Isselee/SS; 24 (CTR RT), Kwiatek7/SS; 24 (LO CTR), talseN/SS; 24 (LO LE), Howard Sandler/SS; 24 (LO RT), Marina Jay/SS; 25 (UP LE), anekoho/SS; 25 (UP CTR), Frans Lanting/National Geographic Creative; 25 (UP RT), Eric Isselee/SS; 25 (UP RT), Joseph Scott Photography/SS; 25 (CTR), Denis Tabler/SS; 25 (CTR LE), panbazil/SS; 25 (CTR RT), Aleksey Stemmer/SS; 25 (LO LE), Seleznev Oleg/SS; 25 (LO RT), Andrey Pavlov/SS; 26 (CTR RT), Danny Smythe/SS; 26 (LO LE), Jurand/SS; 26 (LO RT), Kuttly/SS; 26-27, Musée Bonnat, Bayonne, France/The Bridgeman Art Library; 26 (UP LE), Art Resource, NY; 27 (UP RT), Cheryl E. Davis/SS; 27 (UP RT), Nature Art/SS; 27 (UP CTR), design56/SS; 27 (LO RT), MNI/SS; 27 (LO RT), Jjustas/SS; 28 (LO LE), graphixmania/SS; 28-29, jsp/SS; 30 (UP CTR), leungchopan/SS; 30 (UP RT), Peter Dennis/Dorling Kindersley RF/Getty Images; 30 (LO LE), MiloVad/SS; 30 (LO CTR), kzww/SS; 30 (CTR RT), Mary Evans Picture Library/Alamy; 30 (LO LE), Aleksandar Mijatovic/SS; 31 (UP LE), Cameraphoto Arte Venezia/The Bridgeman Art Library; 31 (UP RT), Eric Isselee/SS; 31 (UP CTR), dwori/SS; 31 (LO CTR), Igor Chernomorchenko/SS; 31 (LO RT), Viachaslau Kraskouski/SS; 32 (LO RT), kangshutters/SS; 32 (CTR LE), North Wind Picture Archives/Alamy; 32-33, claudiodelfuoco/Moment Open/Getty Images; 32 (CTR LE), Art Directors & TRIP/Alamy; 32 (CTR RT), 2HotBrazil/iStockphoto; 33 (UP RT), Scisetti Alfio/SS; 33 (LO RT), Hanan Isachar/Alamy; 34 (CTR LE), Potapov Alexander/SS; 34 (LO RT), Mediagram/SS; 34 (CTR RT), Look and Learn/The Bridgeman Art Library; 34 (UP LE), Tischenko Irina/SS; 34, Renata Sedmakova /SS; 35 (UP RT), Africa Studio/SS; 35 (CTR RT), Blend Images/SS; 35 (LO RT), Mary Evans Picture Library/Alamy; 36 (UP LE), kanvag/SS; 36 (LO LE), frescomovie/SS; 36 (CTR RT), SuperStock; 36 (LO RT), De Agostini Picture Library/The Bridgeman Art Library; 36-37, Werner Forman Archive/The Bridgeman Art Library; 37 (UP RT), cosma/SS; 37 (LO RT), psamtik/SS; 37 (UP RT), SuperStock; 37 (LO LE), Lebrecht Music and Arts Photo Library/Alamy; 38 (LO CTR), Tischenko Irina/SS; 38 (LO RT), Sashkin/SS; 38 (UP CTR), Art Directors & TRIP/Alamy: 38 (CTR RT), adoc-photos/Corbis; 38 (LO CTR), Bhandol/Alamy; 39 (UP LE), Mary Evans Picture Library/Alamy; 39 (UP CTR), Boule/SS; 39 (LO CTR), North Wind Picture Archives/Alamy; 39 (CTR LE), Art Directors & TRIP/Alamy; 39 (LO LE), oksana2010/SS; 40 (UP CTR), Valentyn Volkov/SS; 40 (UP RT), chiqui/SS; 40 (LO LE), nito/SS; 40 (LO RT), Irina Afonskaya/SS; 40 (LO LE), PRISMA ARCHIVO/Alamy; 41 (UP LE), roundstripe/SS; 41 (UP CTR), Sunteya/SS; 41 (UP RT), Shawn Hempel/SS; 41 (LO CTR), blueeyes/SS; 41 (CTR RT), picturepartners/SS; 41 (LO RT), marilyn barbone/SS; 42 (UP LE),Tristan3D/SS; 42 (CTR RT), Kunkie99/SS; 42 (LO LE), Eric Isselee/SS; 42-43, LilKar/SS; 42 (UP CTR), Heritage Image Partnership Ltd./Alamy; 42 (CTR RT), The Art Archive/Gianni Dagli Orti/Art Resource, NY; 43 (UP RT), LanKS/SS; 43 (CTR RT), Francois Loubser/SS; 43 (CTR LE), Scruggelgreen/SS; 44 (LO RT), George Dukinas/SS; 44 (LO CTR), www.BibleLandPictures.com/Alamy; 44 (UP RT), www.BibleLandPictures.com/Alamy; 44 (UP CTR), Art Directors & TRIP/Alamy; 44 (UP RT), www.BibleLandPictures.com/Alamy; 44 (CTR LE), www.BibleLandPictures.com/Alamy; 45 (CTR RT), paul prescott/SS; 45 (LO RT), Michele Falzone/Alamy; 45 (UP CTR), De Agostini Picture Library/The Bridgeman Art Library; 45 (UP LE), Look and Learn/The Bridgeman Art Library; 45 (LO CTR), Look and Learn/The Bridgeman Art Library; 45 (LO CTR), Nir Alon/Alamy; 46-47, Richard Peterson/SS; 48 (UP RT), koya979/SS; 48 (CTR RT), Renata Sedmakova/SS; 48 (CTR RT), HeinSchlebusch/SS; 48 (LO LE), StevenRussellSmithPhotos/SS; 48 (LO RT), Fedorov Oleksiy/SS; 49 (LO LE), koya979/SS; 49 (UP LE), INTERFOTO/Alamy; 49 (UP RT), Archives Charmet/The Bridgeman Art Library; 49 (CTR LE), Muzeum Narodowe, Gdansk, Poland/The Bridgeman Art Library; 49 (CTR RT), World History Archive/Alamy; 50 (UP LE), Hintau Aliaksei/SS; 50 (CTR RT), J. Lekavicius/SS; 50 (CTR LE), John Copland/SS; 50-51, Niday Picture Library/Alamy; 51 (UP CTR), Shawn Hempel/SS; 51 (CTR RT), Copit/SS; 51 (LO RT), Colin McConnell/Toronto Star/Getty Images; 52 (CTR LE), Tsekhmister/ SS; 52 (UP RT), Carolyn Franks/SS; 52 (LO RT), INTERFOTO/Alamy; 52-53, Metropolitan Museum of Art, New York, USA/The Bridgeman Art Library; 53 (UP LE), jorisvo/SS; 53 (UP RT), Todd Bolen/BiblePlaces.com; 53 (CTR RT), Ilya Shapovalov/SS; 53 (CTR LE), tanuha2001/SS; 53 (LO RT), Maksim Dubinsky/SS; 54 (UP LE), Vereshchagin Dmitry/SS; 54 (CTR RT), Horiyan/SS; 54 (UP RT), Look and Learn/The Bridgeman Art Library; 54 (CTR RT), www.BibleLandPictures.com/Alamy; 54 (UP CTR), Zev Radovan/The Bridgeman Art Library; 54 (CTR LE), Mondadori Portfolio/Electa/Sergio Anelli/The Bridgeman Art Library; 54 (UP CTR), Classic Image/Alamy; 55 (LO RT), clearviewstock/SS; 55 (LO CTR), Museo della Collegiata di Sant'Andrea, Empoli, Italy/The Bridgeman Art Library; 55 (UP RT), www.lyre-of-ur.com; 55 (LO CTR), Kues/SS; 55 (UP LE), Look and Learn/The Bridgeman Art Library; 56 (LO LE), Tischenko Irina/SS; 56-57, Mitsuhiko Imamori/Minden Pictures//Corbis; 58 (UP LE), Lebrecht Music and Arts Photo Library/Alamy; 58-59, Alinari/The Bridgeman Art Library; 58 (CTR LE), PRISMA ARCHIVO /Alamy; 58 (LO LE), Look and Learn/The Bridgeman Art Library; 59 (UP RT), Alexey A. Belikov/SS; 59 (CTR LE), videodoctor/SS; 59 (UP LE), The Art Gallery Collection/Alamy; 59 (LO RT), Alinari/The Bridgeman Art Library; 60 (LO LE), albund/SS; 60 (UP LE), Robert Neumann/Alamy; 60 (CTR RT), The Print Collector/Alamy; 60-61, Cosmo Condina Middle East/Alamy; 61 (CTR RT), Russell Kord/Alamy; 61 (UP RT), Archives Charmet/The Bridgeman Art Library; 61 (LO LE), Art Directors & TRIP/Alamy; 61 (LO LE), LittleStocker/SS; 62, SS; 62 (UP RT), Ansis Klucis/SS; 62 (LO RT), The Art Archive/Kharbine-Tapabor/Art Resource, NY; 62-63, The Art Archive/Gianni Dagli Orti/Art Resource, NY; 63 (UP LE), Tatiana Popova/SS; 63 (UP RT), Idealink Photography/Alamy; 63 (UP CTR), Rafael Valls Gallery, London, UK/The Bridgeman Art Library; 63 (LO LE), Look and Learn/Rosenberg Collection/The Bridgeman Art Library; 64 (CTR LE), Seregam/SS; 64 (CTR LE), Artem Samokhvalov/SS; 64 (LO RT), Hong Vo/SS; 64-65, JLImages/Alamy; 64 (UP RT), Timewatch Images/Alamy; 65 (UP RT), Sukharevskyy Dmytro /SS; 65 (CTR LE), Eric Isselee/SS; 65 (LO CTR), artproem/SS; 65 (LO CTR), PhotoHouse/SS; 65 (LO RT), Bernd Juergens/SS; 66 (LO LE), Smit/SS; 66-67, Konstantin Chagin/SS; 68 (UP LE), telesniuk/SS; 68-69, PRISMA ARCHIVO/Alamy; 68 (CTR RT), Superstock; 68 (LO LE), Kristina Birukova/SS; 69 (LO RT), DnD-Production.com/SS; 69 (UP LE), FineArt/Alamy; 69 (CTR LE), Giraudon/The Bridgeman Art Library; 69 (UP RT), alexsl/iStockphoto; 70 (CTR LE), Heritage Image Partnership Ltd./Alamy; 70 (LO LE), The Granger Collection, NYC; 70-71, Banana Republic images/SS; 71 (LO RT), www.BibleLandPictures.com/Alamy; 71 (UP RT), Natalia Paklina/SS; 71 (CTR RT), jovan vitanovski/SS; 72 (LO LE), Greg Balfour Evans/Alamy; 72-73, Stuart Dee/Photographer's Choice/Getty Images; 72 (UP LE), Sonia Halliday Photographs /Alamy; 72 (CTR RT), Albright-Knox Art Gallery/Corbis; 73 (UP RT), Leemage/Corbis; 73 (CTR RT), AF archive/Alamy; 73 (LO LE), Album/Art Resource, NY; 74 (UP RT), Maridav/SS; 74 (CTR LE), Sergej Razvodovskij/SS; 74 (LO CTR), RTimages/SS; 74 (LO CTR), Cre8tive Studios /Alamy; 74 (UP LE), Mary Evans Picture Library/Alamy; 74 (UP CTR), amana images inc./Alamy; 74 (CTR RT), Roland Pargeter/Alamy; 74 (LO RT), andamanec/SS; 75 (UP RT), Vasiliy Vishnevskiy/Alamy; 75 (LO RT), GFC Collection/Alamy; 75 (UP LE), Eric Isselee/SS; 75 (LO CTR), Bernd Schmidt/SS; 75 (LO CTR), Elena Schweitzer/SS; 75 (LO LE), itakefotos4u/SS; 76 (UP RT), MANDY GODBEHEAR/SS; 76 (LO RT), Nero diVenere/SS; 76 (CTR LE), Classic Image/Alamy; 76-77, FineArt/Alamy; 77 (UP RT), Gurkan Erenler/Art Resource, NY; 77 (CTR LE), De Agostini Picture Library/G. Nimatallah/The Bridgeman Art Library; 77 (LO LE), DenisNata/SS; 78 (UP LE), DVARG/SS; 78 (UP CTR), Michael Leslie/SS; 78 (UP RT), germanjames/SS; 78 (LO CTR), antpkr/SS; 78 (LO LE), Butterfly Hunter/SS; 78-79, URRRA/SS; 79 (CTR RT), bogdan ionescu/SS; 79 (LO LE), Stephen Coburn/SS; 79 (CTR RT), branislavpudar/SS; 79 (LO RT), Studio DMM Photography, Designs & Art/SS; 80 (UP CTR), Marina Jay/SS; 80 (LO LE), pzAxe/SS; 80 (UP RT), Mary Evans Picture Library/Alamy; 80 (LO CTR), De Agostini Picture Library/Gianni Dagli Orti/The Granger Collection, NYC; 80 (LO RT), Mary Evans Picture Library/Alamy; 81 (CTR RT), The Granger Collection, NYC; 81 (UP LE), North Wind Picture Archives/Alamy; 81 (LO RT), Mike Flippo/SS; 81 (LO LE), Gannet77/iStockphoto; 81 (LO RT), Brooklyn Museum of Art, New York, USA/The Bridgeman Art Library; 82 (LO CTR), Mary Evans Picture Library/Alamy; 82 (UP LE), DeskyCom/SS; 82 (CTR RT), Bombaert Patrick/SS; 82 (UP RT), Giraudon/The Bridgeman Art Library; 82 (LO LE), PRISMA ARCHIVO/Alamy; 83 (LO RT), jozef sedmak/Alamy; 83 (UP CTR), Svetlana Lukienko/SS; 83 (CTR RT), Hannamariah/SS; 83 (CTR LE), Ana Martinez de Mingo/SS; 83 (LO LE), John Copland/SS; 84 (UP LE), Evlakhov Valeriy/SS; 84 (UP RT), Mega Pixel/SS; 84 (UP CTR), The Art Archive/Gianni Dagli Orti/Art Resource, NY; 84 (LO LE), The Granger Collection, NYC; 84 (LO RT), Giraudon/The Bridgeman Art Library; 84-85, binik/SS; 85 (UP LE), Alex Staroseltsev/SS; 85 (UP CTR), pukach/SS; 85 (LO CTR), harmpeti/SS; 85 (LO CTR), Picsfive/SS; 86 (UP CTR), Heritage Image Partnership Ltd./Alamy; 86 (LO LE), Mary Evans Picture Library/Alamy; 86-87, Nancy Bauer/SS; 87 (UP RT), Holmes Garden Photos/Alamy; 87 (CTR RT), koya979/SS; 87 (LO LE), The Art Gallery Collection/Alamy; 87 (UP LE), Mondadori Portfolio/Electa/Sergio Anelli/The Bridgeman Art Library; 90 (CTR RT), Lebrecht Music and Arts Photo Library/Alamy; 90 (LO LE), Mary Evans Picture Library/Alamy; 90 (LO RT), Chronicle/Alamy; 90 (CTR LE), Renata Sedmakova/SS; 90 (UP RT), Renata Sedmakova/SS; 91 (CTR LE), Zvonimir Atletic/SS; 91 (UP CTR), Renata Sedmakova/SS; 91 (UP LE), Giraudon/The Bridgeman Art Library; 91 (UP RT), Renata Sedmakova/SS; 91 (LO LE), Look and Learn/The Bridgeman Art Library; 91 (LO RT), Heritage Image Partnership Ltd./Alamy.

STAFF FOR THIS BOOK
Erica Green, *Senior Editor*
Amanda Larsen, *Art Director*
Lori Epstein, *Senior Photo Editor*
Paige Towler, *Editorial Assistant*
Sanjida Rashid, *Design Production Assistant*
Michael Cassady, *Photo Assistant*
Grace Hill, *Associate Managing Editor*
Joan Gossett, *Production Editor*
Lewis R. Bassford, *Production Manager*
George Bounelis, *Manager, Production Services*
Susan Borke, *Legal and Business Affairs*

PRODUCED BY POTOMAC GLOBAL MEDIA, LLC
Project Team:
Kevin Mulroy, *Publisher*
Barbara Brownell Grogan, *Editor/Project Manager*
Carol Farrar Norton, *Art Director*
David Hicks, *Picture Editor*
Karin Kinney, *Research Editor*
Jane Sunderland, *Consulting Editor*
Robin Currie, Jill Rubalcaba, *Contributing Writers*
Robert Cargill, Eric Cline, Tammi Schneider, *Consultants*

PUBLISHED BY THE NATIONAL GEOGRAPHIC SOCIETY
Gary E. Knell, *President and CEO*
John M. Fahey, *Chairman of the Board*
Melina Gerosa Bellows, *Chief Education Officer*
Declan Moore, *Chief Media Officer*
Hector Sierra, *Senior Vice President and General Manager, Book Division*

SENIOR MANAGEMENT TEAM, KIDS PUBLISHING AND MEDIA
Nancy Laties Feresten, *Senior Vice President*
Jennifer Emmett, *Vice President, Editorial Director, Kids Books*
Julie Vosburgh Agnone, *Vice President, Editorial Operations*
Rachel Buchholz, *Editor and Vice President*, NG Kids *magazine*
Michelle Sullivan, *Vice President, Kids Digital*
Eva Absher-Schantz, *Design Director*
Jay Sumner, *Photo Director*
Hannah August, *Marketing Director*
R. Gary Colbert, *Production Director*

DIGITAL
Anne McCormack, *Director*
Laura Goertzel, Sara Zeglin, *Producers*
Jed Winer, *Special Projects Assistant*
Emma Rigney, *Creative Producer*
Brian Ford, *Video Producer*
Bianca Bowman, *Assistant Producer*
Natalie Jones, *Senior Product Manager*

The National Geographic Society is one of the world's largest nonprofit scientific and educational organizations. Founded in 1888 to "increase and diffuse geographic knowledge," the Society's mission is to inspire people to care about the planet. It reaches more than 400 million people worldwide each month through its official journal, *National Geographic*, and other magazines; National Geographic Channel; television documentaries; music; radio; films; books; DVDs; maps; exhibitions; live events; school publishing programs; interactive media; and merchandise. National Geographic has funded more than 10,000 scientific research, conservation, and exploration projects and supports an education program promoting geographic literacy.

For more information, please visit nationalgeographic.com, call 1-800-NGS LINE (647-5463), or write to the following address:
National Geographic Society
1145 17th Street N.W.
Washington, D.C. 20036-4688 U.S.A.

Visit us online at nationalgeographic.com/books

For librarians and teachers: ngchildrensbooks.org

More for kids from National Geographic: kids.nationalgeographic.com

For information about special discounts for bulk purchases, please contact National Geographic Books Special Sales: ngspecsales@ngs.org

For rights or permissions inquiries, please contact National Geographic Books Subsidiary Rights: ngbookrights@ngs.org

Hardcover ISBN: 978-1-4263-1865-8
Reinforced library binding ISBN: 978-1-4263-1866-5

Printed in the United States of America
14/WOR/1